Bible Studies
Galatians to Philemon

Second Edition

James Malm

ISBN: 978-1-7753510-0-9
Copyright © 2019 James David Malm
All Rights Reserved

Dedication

This work is dedicated to the Great God whose house is eternity; the Father and Sovereign of all that exists and the sum of all Truth, Wisdom, Love, Justice and Mercy.
May God's house be filled with children whose chief joy is to be like Him!

Visit Our Website
theshininglight.info

Table of Contents

Galatians **7**
    Galatians 1 8
    Galatians 2 14
    Galatians 3 23
    Galatians 4 36
    Galatians 5 43
    Galatians 6 50

Ephesians **55**
    Ephesians 1 56
    Ephesians 2 62
    Ephesians 3 68
    Ephesians 4 71
    Ephesians 5 79
    Ephesians 6 88

Philippians **93**
    Philippians 1 94
    Philippians 2 99
    Philippians 3 104
    Philippians 4 108

Colossians **113**
    Colossians 1 114
    Colossians 2 120
    Colossians 3 127
    Colossians 4 132

First Thessalonians **135**
    1 Thessalonians 1 136
    1 Thessalonians 2 140
    1 Thessalonians 3 143
    1 Thessalonians 4 146
    1 Thessalonians 5 150

Second Thessalonians **163**

    2 Thessalonians 1 164

    2 Thessalonians 2 167

    2 Thessalonians 3 172

First Timothy **175**

    1 Timothy 1 176

    1 Timothy 2 180

    1 Timothy 3 183

    1 Timothy 4 190

    1 Timothy 5 193

    1 Timothy 6 198

Second Timothy **201**

    2 Timothy 1 202

    2 Timothy 2 206

    2 Timothy 3 212

    2 Timothy 4 216

Titus **219**

    Titus 1 220

    Titus 2 224

    Titus 3 227

Philemon **231**

    Philemon 232

Galatians

Galatians 1

The Epistles of Paul have been attacked and twisted from the very days of Paul himself. Today they are twisted and perverted so as to appear to mean the exact opposite of what they do mean, turning Paul's teachings to keep God's Word with passionate zeal into an excuse to minimize and compromise with the law and the Word of God.

While Alexander spread Hellenism with his conquests, Aristotle was the tutor of Alexander and the author of Hellenism which is merely Aristotelian logic; and modern Transformative Education is merely the logic of Aristotle; which is the foundation of modern Rabbinic Judaism and Catholic based professing Christianity.

This logic starts off with a reasonable appearing but false premise and then uses often beautiful logic to come to an erroneous conclusion.

To begin, a careful study through the scriptures and especially the Epistles of Paul is essential to ground the brethren in the sound doctrine of Holy Scripture and protect them from the attempts of wicked men to lead them astray.

Watch that PREMISE! If the opening assumption [the premise] is wrong; then good logic will reach a wrong conclusion. Always watch that premise!

In Galatians Chapter 1 Paul introduces his subject.

To understand the various epistles, it is necessary to understand who they are written to and to understand a little something about the subject and the times.

The book of Galatians was written to the people of the Greek province of Galatia. Among these people were Gentiles who knew nothing about the things of God until they were converted and certain Jews also lived among these Gentiles. And these Jews wanted the Galatians to be circumcised in order to be integrated into the Mosaic Covenant, not fully understanding the spiritual circumcision of the New Covenant.

Paul was writing on the subject of circumcision, to point out the meaning of circumcision, and to point out the spiritual New Covenant meaning of the subject of circumcision.

Galatians 1:1 Paul, an apostle, not called of men, neither by man, but by Jesus Christ and God the Father, who raised him, [raised Jesus Christ] from the dead.

Paul says that he was not appointed to serve [was not ordained] by any man, but was called directly by God the Father and by Jesus Christ. He was not ordained by any man.

Those who idolize ordination by men should listen to Paul here. He says that he was not ordained or called or chosen by any man, but was called directly by God the Father and Jesus Christ.

Nearly all men who were ordained by other men have proved out to be ungodly men because they were not ordained according to the scriptures, but ordained for their loyalty to other men.

Now of course, if God should COMMAND a man to ordain a specific person for a specific responsibility or as their successor; God should be obeyed.

A major question is who should be ordained and the answer is that no man should be ordained until and unless God makes it very clear that the person is God's choice; at that point the ordaining is only a public acceptance of what God has already decided.

People should only be ordained according to God's criteria.

No one should be ordained because of a college or seminary education, no person should be ordained who does not meet the scriptural requirements for ordination being of full age and well experienced in life and in the faith; having been married and raised up children, BEFORE any ordination.

1:2 And all the brethren which are with me unto the churches of Galatia: 1:3 Grace be to you and peace from God the Father, and from our Lord Jesus Christ, 1:4 Who gave himself for our sins that he might deliver us from this present evil world, according to the will of God and our Father, 1:5 To whom be glory for ever and ever. Amen.

Paul was astonished that they had so quickly turned away from the spiritual New Covenant.

1:6 I marvel that you are so soon removed from him that called you into the grace of Christ, unto another gospel.

Paul is amazed that they [and we also] are turning away from the gospel of Christ; turning away from the true gospel of sincere repentance and zeal to live as Christ lived and lives; in passionate zeal to keep every Word of God: being perverted into a false gospel of a tolerant for sin false Jesus Christ.

1:7 But this is not another; but there be some that trouble you, and would pervert the gospel of Christ. 1:8 But though we, or an angel from heaven, preach any other gospel unto you than that which we have preached unto you, let him be accursed. 1:9 As we said before, so say I now again; if any man preach any other gospel unto you than that you have received, let him be accursed.

There is only one true gospel which is the Gospel of Salvation through sincere repentance, baptism, the application of the sacrifice of Christ and an unshakable commitment to live by Word of God.

Paul pronounces a curse on anyone who changes from the doctrines that were originally preached by Jesus Christ and later by Paul. Paul said, I told you the truth [God's Word is truth]. Therefore, let anyone who is perverting that truth be accursed.

This curse is on all those who follow the LIE that we are to blindly and unquestioningly follow whatever men say and are not to be zealous to live by every Word God, and those who teach the LIE that Jesus Christ is tolerant of any sin.

John 17:17 Sanctify them through thy truth: thy word is truth.

Galatians 1:10 For do I now persuade men, or God? Or do I seek to please men? For if I yet pleased men, I should not be the servant of Christ.

Paul said, I am not trying to please either the Jews or the Gentiles. I am pleasing God. I am a servant of Jesus Christ and what I am telling you is the truth of God the Father and Jesus Christ and is for everyone, not for the benefit of any particular group, either Jew or Gentile. It is the truth and the gospel of God the Father and Jesus Christ.

1:11 But I certify you, brethren, that **the gospel, which was preached of me is not after man. 1:12 But I neither received it of man, neither was I taught it, but by the revelation of Jesus Christ.**

Paul clearly says that these things were revealed directly to him from Jesus Christ. Paul was not taught these things by Peter or James or John or any of the other apostles or disciples. Paul learned and understood these things through the direct inspiration and teaching of Jesus Christ.

Those who accept the Primacy of Peter heresy, the false doctrine that Peter was the chief apostle, and that God only works through one man, should ask themselves why Christ did not use Peter to teach Paul.

Why did Jesus Christ directly call teach and inspire Paul, and teach Paul these things? why did Jesus not reveal these things to Paul through Peter? I think that is a valid question for those who stand by the Primacy of Peter teaching.

1:13 For you have heard of my conversation or conduct in past time in the Jews' religion, how that beyond measure I persecuted the church of God, and wasted it: **1:14** And profited in the Jews' religion above many my equals in mine own nation, being more exceedingly zealous for the traditions of my fathers. **1:15** but when it pleased God, who separated me from my mother's womb, and called me by his grace, **1:16** To reveal his Son in me, that I might preach him among the heathen; immediately I conferred not with flesh and blood.

Paul appeals to the Jews and tells them how very zealous he was for the Mosaic Covenant and for the religion of his people, the religion of the Mosaic Pharisees. He said, I was very zealous for these things, I know them, I understand them; and I know where you guys are coming from; but when I was struck down in the flesh, I immediately conferred, not with flesh and blood, but with the resurrected to spirit Jesus Christ.

Jesus was changed to a spirit, at his resurrection he became a spirit and he appeared to Paul on the road to Damascus. So, Paul was not then conversing with flesh and blood, with human beings; but with the real Spirit Jesus Christ.

He did not receive this inspiration or this understanding or this knowledge from Peter or any of the other apostles. He received it directly from the resurrected Jesus Christ.

1:17 Neither went I up to Jerusalem unto those, which were apostles before me; but I went into Arabia, and returned again to Damascus.

Paul was struck down, and as we know in the book of Acts, he went to Damascus where he received his sight back in part and after a time, he went to Arabia and then he returned to Damascus. This does NOT say that Paul was in Arabia for three years as some have wrongly taught.

Paul writes that he went up to Jerusalem three years after he returned to Damascus from Arabia, which means that Paul was in Damascus for three years after returning from Arabia before going to Jerusalem.

1:18 And then, after three years, I went up to Jerusalem to see Peter and abode with him 15 days.

Paul stayed in Damascus for three years AFTER he returned there from Arabia, the time in Arabia is not stated.

Paul says that he did not even speak to Peter until more than three years after he saw Christ and he also did not speak to any of the other apostles until he had gone to Jerusalem after more than three years.

1:19 But others of the apostles saw I none, except James the Lord's brother. **1:20** Now, the things which I write to you, behold, before God, I do not lie. **1:21** afterwords I came into the regions of Syria and Cilicia; **1:22** And was unknown by face unto the churches of Judea which were in Christ.

After spending three years in Damascus after returning from an unknown time in Arabia, Paul went to Jerusalem and spent 15 days with Peter and visited with James and then left Judea and went to Syria and Cilicia. He was still unknown by personal appearance or by his face to the people of the Ekklesia in Judea which were in Christ.

Paul emphasized to the Jews and to the Gentiles in Galatia that he was inspired and taught by the resurrected Jesus Christ directly, and was not taught through Peter, or James, or John, or anybody else.

That says a lot about this idea that Peter was the chief apostle, and that God only works through one man, which is simply not true! God works through whomever God wants, whenever God wants, wherever God wants and in whatever way God wants.

1:23 But they that had heard only, That he which persecuted us in past times now preaches the faith which once he attacked and destroyed. **1:24** And they glorified God in me.

More than 3 years after seeing Christ on the road to Damascus, and then 15 days in Jerusalem, and then after another 14 years, Paul went back to Jerusalem a second time.

Paul was called directly by God and was NOT ordained by any man, and God used this non-ordained by man person to write a very large part of the New Testament.

Galatians 2

Paul goes into a short history of his calling and ministry to establish that he learned the Word directly from Christ and that he did not learn the New Covenant doctrine from other men, nor was he ordained by men, but was called and ordained directly by God.

Then Paul immediately goes into the Doctrine of Salvation by Jesus Christ; which doctrine is being rejected by those who are perverting the sacrifice of Christ into a license and excuse to compromise with the Word of God.

Galatians 2:1 Then fourteen years after I went up again to Jerusalem with Barnabas, and took Titus with me also.

2:2 And I went up by revelation [Paul was inspired by God to go to Jerusalem], and communicated unto the people there the gospel which I preach among the Gentiles, but privately to them which were of reputation, lest by any means I should run, or had run, in vain.

Paul reveals that he spent some time in Damascus, then more time in the wilderness of Arabia, followed by three years in Damascus and only then spends just 15 days in Jerusalem; and then after that it was another 14 years before he went back to Jerusalem.

When he returned to Jerusalem, Paul sought out and communicated in private with the leaders of the brethren. The second trip to Jerusalem was made to see whether they were still on the same page and whether they were all teaching the same things, so that he could determine whether he had run or taught anything in vain.

Paul certainly does not mean to imply that he went to them for any permissions or corrections from them; rather this was an exchange of information about what he was doing in his area and what these men were doing in Jerusalem, as well as a discussion of spiritual matters in an "iron sharpens iron" discussion, as any group of believers should have.

These men would have benefited from communicating with each other: That does NOT mean or imply any kind of subordinate role by anyone. In fact, everyone would mutually benefit from such an exchange of information.

2:3 But neither Titus, who was with me, being a Greek, was compelled to be circumcised,

Then, some sought to compel Titus to be circumcised and Paul rejected their demands.

2:4 And that, because of false brethren unawares brought in, who secretly came in to privily or secretly **spy out our liberty which we have in Christ Jesus, that they might bring us into bondage: 2:5 To whom we gave place by subjection, no, not for an hour.**

Paul did not submit to these people. Paul was very strong to bow only to God and not to any man; following men ONLY as they follow God the Father and Jesus Christ just as we all should be doing!

2:6 But of these who seemed to be somewhat, whatsoever they were, it makes no matter to me, it means nothing to me for God does not accept any man's person. . .

The brethren should remember that God accepts no man's person and that each of us must prove all things by every Word of God.

What really matters is whether what people say is consistent with the Word of God, and whether they practice what they say.

Paul says that it made no matter to him who a person is or what title he claims, for God accepts no man's person above another.

If a man is wrong, then God will correct him no matter WHO he thinks he is. We are ALL held to the same standard; the Word and Law of God.

If you stand before Jesus Christ at your judgment and he asks you why you called his Sabbath holy and still polluted it, and if you answer that you followed the teachings of some man; Jesus Christ will say that the sin of idolatry has been added to your list of wickedness and Jesus Christ will cast you away!

> **Matthew 7:23** And then will I profess unto them, I never knew you: depart from me, ye that work iniquity.

Galatians 2:6 . . . For they that seemed to be somewhat in conference added nothing to me: **2:7** But contrariwise, when they saw that the gospel of the uncircumcision [preaching to the Gentiles of Europe and Asia Minor] was committed unto me, as the gospel of the circumcision [preaching to the Jews in Judea] was committed to Peter; **2:8** For he that wrought effectually in Peter to the apostleship of the circumcision or of the Jews, the same was mighty in me toward the Gentiles.

This is not quite so simple as Jews in Palestine and Gentiles elsewhere; for Jesus Christ through the Holy Spirit was doing a great work in Peter and others with both the Jews and Gentiles in Palestine: And the same Holy Spirit of Jesus Christ was doing a mighty work in Paul toward the Jews [most of whom rejected the way] and to the Gentiles in Europe and Asia Minor.

Christ also did a work in India by Thomas and in other places through other men. Each man had his assignment and although they tried to communicate to make sure that they were on the same page spiritually and had not drifted; each was answerable to Jesus Christ who was the Chief Apostle.

The Chief Apostle of our salvation is Jesus Christ and NOT any man!

> **Hebrews 3:1** Wherefore, holy brethren, partakers of the heavenly calling, **consider the Apostle and High Priest of our profession, Christ Jesus; 3:2** Who was faithful to him that appointed him [faithful to God the Father]

Galatians 2:9 And when James, and Cephas, [Peter], and John, who seemed to be pillars, perceived the grace [When they understood that Paul had a commission from God for Asia Minor and Europe.] that was given to me, they gave to me and Barnabas the right hands of fellowship; that we should go unto the heathen, and they unto the circumcision.

Notice here that Peter and James and John were not jealous of Paul and they didn't say, oh no God only works through us. They said, it looks like God is doing something in you and we are giving you the hands of friendship and we support you and will help you and cooperate with you and let's work together.

They were not jealous, and egocentric like many in today's spiritual Ekklesia. God does not work through just one person. God is obviously working through all of them and they rejoiced to see the wonderful things that Christ was doing in also sending salvation to the Gentiles in Europe and Asia Minor.

2:10 Only that they wanted that we should remember the poor; the same thing which I also was forward to do. **2:11** But **when Peter was come to Antioch, there I withstood him to the face, because he was to be blamed and to be resisted**. **2:12** For before that certain came from James, he did eat with the Gentiles: but when they were come from James, he withdrew and separated himself, fearing them which were of the circumcision or of the Jews.

Did you get that? Did you hear that? You people who are into the Primacy of Peter, you people who think God works through one man only, and that some man has the right to do whatever he wants; Paul resisted God's apostle Peter; because he was wrong!

Paul withstood him to his face, saying, you are wrong sir, and what you are doing is wrong.

No, Peter was not the chief apostle. They were all working together and they were all inspired by God. God is building a tremendous spiritual building, a temple which is his Ekklesia, his people and Jesus Christ is the Master Builder, not any man.

Jesus Christ has many tools, and the various true apostles, and true prophets, and true evangelists, and so on are only tools in the hands of God. True men of God would acknowledge that, and they would acknowledge God's authority over them, and they would acknowledge that Almighty God can use whatever tool he wants to, in whatever way God wants.

Yes, Paul withstood Peter because certain disciples came to Antioch and immediately Peter thought, "I better be very careful here about what I do with these Gentiles, because I might offend these Jews." And Paul withstood him over that kind of duplicity.

Let's understand what was actually going on here. Under the Mosaic Covenant, the Jews would not have anything to do with the Gentiles, because the Gentiles might render them unclean in some way, being uncircumcised. In Judea at this time, Gentiles were not invited into a Jewish home. A Jew did not go into a Gentile's home. They did not generally associate with one another.

The only way that there could be an association, is if a Gentile was circumcised and committed himself to the Mosaic Covenant. In that case, this Gentile was grafted into Israel. He became a Mosaic Jew, and no longer was considered a Gentile. He was grafted into Israel.

We can find this commandment in:

> **Exodus 12:48** And when a stranger shall sojourn with thee, and will keep the Passover to the LORD, let all his males be circumcised, and then let him come near and keep it; and he shall be as one that is born in the land: for no uncircumcised person shall eat thereof.

The fact is, the Jews did not associate with physically uncircumcised Gentiles. And yet Peter was associating with fleshly uncircumcised Gentiles called out into the New Covenant UNTIL some Jewish visitors came, and Peter thought that he had better not associate with these Gentiles anymore because it might offend the Jewish brethren.

Peter was respecting one race above another which is contrary to the New Covenant in which all races are called into a single spiritual organism and there is no race, except the race of Godliness. Paul continues this through Galatians 3.

Galatians 2:13 And the other Jews which were among us dissembled likewise with him; insomuch that Barnabas himself was carried away with their dissimulation.

Then the other local Jews got upset about associating with uncircumcised Gentiles who had been called into the New Covenant and were circumcised in the heart and they begin to separate themselves from the Gentile converts, because they had not been circumcised in the flesh according to the Mosaic Covenant.

2:14 But when I, [that is Paul]; saw that they walked not uprightly according to the truth of the gospel, I said unto Peter before them all, If you, being a Jew, live after the manner of Gentiles.

That is, these men were not so concerned with all of these Jewish traditions like fasting on certain days of the week and so on, which were traditions of the Pharisees.

Paul asks them, if you are not concerned about the traditions of the Pharisees anymore and you live similarly to the New Covenant Gentiles and you do not live as the Pharisees did, according to their traditions why are you beginning to ostracize your brethren?

. . . why compellest you the Gentiles to live as do the Jews?

Now Paul goes into the need to keep the law of God in the New Covenant and that it is wrong to reject other brethren in the New Covenant who are now circumcised in heart.

2:15 We who are Jews by nature [physical Mosaic Israel now being converted into New Covenant spiritual Israel], and not sinners of the Gentiles, **2:16** knowing that a man is not justified by the works of the law, [That is; the deeds and traditions of men, or any future law keeping; does not atone for PAST sins.] but is justified by the faith of Jesus Christ, even we have believed in Jesus Christ, that we might be justified by the faith of Christ, and not by the works of the law: for by the works of the law shall no flesh be justified.

No flesh, no person; can be justified before God for their past deeds of sin by any future law keeping. That is because ALL have sinned at some point and even if we keep the law perfectly after that, we must still pay for that PAST sin and NO amount of future law abiding can atone for past sin.

For example if you murder someone and then live perfectly for many years; you are still a murderer.

We can keep all kinds of traditions and fast three days week and avoid associating with physically uncircumcised yet converted New Covenant Gentiles, which is the subject here: And that is not going to justify anyone.

People can only be justified by sincere repentance, a genuine baptismal commitment to go and sin no more, and faith in the application of the atoning sacrifice of Jesus Christ, which is circumcision of the heart!

No matter how perfectly the law is kept in future it still does not atone for PAST sin.

We can wake up today, and say we are going to be perfect from here on out forever. But that doesn't pay for our previous sins!

To have those PAST sins paid for and be reconciled to God, only comes through sincere repentance and faith in the sacrifice of Jesus Christ.

Paul says, you can't be justified, you can't be made right with God; by your own deeds. You can only be made right with God by having the sacrifice of Jesus Christ applied to you; and then going forward to diligently do the DEEDS of God; living by every Word of God in future!

The sacrifice of Christ is only APPLIED to the REPENTANT; to those who STOP sinning; it is sincere repentance to stop sinning and the application of the atonement of Christ for our past sins; which justifies and purifies us.

After that, we are to go forward; avoiding sin and living by every Word of God: But keeping the commandments does not justify anyone from PAST sins. It is sacrifice of Christ which justifies us and makes us right with God and atones for our past sins.

2:17 But if, while we seek to be justified by Christ, we ourselves also are found sinners, [that is, if we continue in sin,] is therefore Christ the minister of sin? God forbid.

Once we are justified by sincere repentance, a baptismal commitment to go and sin no more and faith in the sacrifice of Christ, we are NOT to continue in sin; for Paul said, God forbid that we should continue in sin!

2:18 For if I build again the things, which I destroyed, [that is, if we continue in our sinful nature] I make myself a transgressor.

If we have destroyed our past sinful nature in sincere repentance and baptism, rising up from the grave of baptism a NEW being in Christ and becoming justified by our faith in the sacrifice of Christ; if we then continue in sin we remain transgressors.

2:19 For I through the law am dead to the law, that I might live unto God. 2:20 I am crucified with Christ: nevertheless, I live; yet not I, but Christ liveth in me: and the life which I now live in the flesh I live by the faith of the Son of God, who loved me, and gave himself for me

Jesus Christ was crucified for our sins, and if his sacrifice is applied to us, our old sinful self is also dead because Christ died and the crucifixion and sacrifice of Jesus Christ has paid the penalty for our PAST sincerely repented sin. Therefore we must live by every Word of God through the indwelling power of Christ onward from henceforth and forever more!

Our repentance, our baptismal commitment and faith in Christ and his sacrifice, atones for PAST sin. And the sinful man, our sinful nature is dead and gone, and we rise up new persons in Christ.

Jesus Christ can then dwell in us through the power of God's Holy Spirit, and when he [Christ] is dwelling in us, Christ will do the things he has always done, now doing them within us; that is, he will live by every Word of God and we will live by every Word of God in Christ-like zeal as we are led by the Spirit of Christ.

This is the New Covenant circumcision of the heart:

> **Colossians 2:11** In whom also ye are circumcised with the **circumcision** made without hands, in putting off the body of the sins of the flesh by the **circumcision** of Christ:

God's Spirit is not divided against God. God's Spirit is the Spirit and nature of God. God is not divided against himself; God keeps his own Word and he will keep his own Word while dwelling in us!

Christ says, "I have kept my Father's commandments" and the Holy Spirit of God will empower us and lead us to also keep God's commandments and turn away from all sin.

> **John 15:10** If ye keep my commandments, ye shall abide in my love; even as I have kept my Father's commandments, and abide in his love.

Galatians 2:21 I do not frustrate the grace of God: for if righteousness come by the law, then Christ death is in vain.

If we have sinned and we stop sinning today and live perfectly from this point onward: What about past sins?

Keeping the law from this point forward does not atone for our PAST law breaking.

Only sincere repentance and the application of the sacrifice of Jesus Christ can atone for past law breaking; and then the Holy Spirit will be given to us and will empower us to go forward, putting away all sin and living by every Word of God in the future.

To summarize: We must sincerely repent of all PAST sin and then STOP sinning; then to really get that point across we must make a formal baptismal commitment to stop sinning and destroy our PAST sinful self; going down into the grave of water and destroying the old person of sin, and then rising up out of the water a NEW person in Christ and Christ-like zeal to Live by Every Word of GOD.

Then the atoning sacrifice of Jesus Christ the true Lamb of God, will be applied to us and we must go forward in Christ-like zeal to live by every Word of God through the strength of the ultimate overcomer dwelling in us, henceforth and forever!

>**Romans 2:13** (for not the hearers of the law are just before God, but **the doers of the law shall be justified**.

Physical circumcision is only a symbolic removal of a piece of flesh and avails nothing unless God is obeyed [except that physical circumcision is a prophecy of spiritual circumcision into the New Covenant]; it is the spiritual circumcision of the New Covenant which removes our sins which have separated us from God!

The true doctrine of Salvation through Jesus Christ, is that we must become spiritually circumcised, removing all of the sin which separates us from God the Father through sincere repentance, a baptismal commitment to sin no more and the application of the sacrifice of Jesus Christ the Lamb of God.

Anyone who teaches the false doctrine that we need not be passionately faithful and obedient to the whole Word of God, just as Jesus Christ was and is, teaching that we can tolerate compromise with the Word of God; is teaching that we need not be spiritually circumcised and is an Antichrist!

Galatians 3

Paul condemns racism in the Ekklesia and teaches the difference between physical and spiritual circumcision.

Galatians 3:1 O foolish Galatians, who hath bewitched you, that you should not obey the truth, before whose eyes Jesus Christ hath been evidently set forth, crucified among you? **3:2** This only would I learn of you, Received you the Spirit, [Did the Holy Spirit come by perfect law keeping or by the application of the sacrifice of Christ?] by the works of the law, [Does keeping the commandments in future, atone for PAST sin?] or by the hearing of faith?

Did we receive the Holy Spirit by now starting to keep the commandments; or did the penalty for sin have to be paid first so that we could be reconciled to God?

It is our repentance and faith in Christ's atoning sacrifice which reconciles us to God the Father, which then brings us into a relationship with God the Father and then God will give us his Spirit.

3:3 Are you so foolish? Having begun in the Spirit, are you now made perfect by the acts of the flesh? **3:4** Have you suffered so many things in vain? If it be yet in vain. **3:5** He, theretofore, that ministers to you the Spirit, and works miracles among you, doeth he it by the works of the law, or by the hearing of faith? **3:6** Even as Abraham believed God, and [Abraham obeyed God] it was accounted to him for righteousness. **3:7** Know you therefore that they which are of faith, the same are the children of Abraham.

The subject of the book of Galatians was the problem that some Jewish converts had with associating with some Gentile converts who had been circumcised in heart having sincerely repented of sin; but had not been circumcised in the flesh, which was the sign of the Mosaic Covenant and were not following certain Pharisaic traditions.

That is the subject, and Paul starts talking about being saved by faith, and being forgiven through the atoning sacrifice of Christ and living by faith in Christ, and then keeping the commandments through the indwelling of Christ; to show the difference between physical circumcision and circumcision of the heart.

In fact Paul is explaining the difference between keeping God's Word in future and the need for an atonement for PAST sin.

People who do what Abraham did, being full of faith and marrying that faith to the actions of obedience to the whole Word of God; are Abraham's children.

Galatians 3:7 Know you not therefore that they which are of faith, the same are the children of Abraham."

Paul teaches us that it is not just physical Israel who are the children of Abraham, but it is everyone who has sincerely repented and had the atoning sacrifice of Christ applied to them.

Everyone who commits to obey God the Father in all things and who is then filled with God's Spirit, everyone who is filled with faith in God; all of them, both Jew and Gentile including ALL races, are people of faith and are therefore the children of Abraham.

It is not those who are the physical descendants of Abraham but those who do what Christ teaches and what Abraham did as our example; all those who are like Abraham in faith, words and deeds; are truly Abraham's children. Physical descent means nothing in the New Covenant: Believing and living by every Word of God is all in all!

In Hebrews 12:8 Paul explains that those who will not endure correction are not truly sons at all but bastards. Why does any father correct his children? Why, to mold their behavior into what HE wants it to be; to cause the child to act as the father would have him act.

Therefore if we will not do what Abraham did as our example, Abraham is not truly our father in a spiritual sense; and if we do not obey our Father in heaven, then he is NOT our Father in the spiritual sense; and if we will not keep the whole Word of God our Father in heaven; then we are rebellious children in need of severe correction.

> **Hebrews 12:8** But if ye be without chastisement, whereof all are partakers, then are ye bastards, and not sons.

If we become the children of God our Father in heaven and are reconciled to him in faith; and turn away from all sin to live by every Word of God; we also become reconciled to Abraham and become heirs of the promises made to him.

Paul is trying to heal the rift between certain Jews and certain Gentiles in saying that if we have faith in God and in Christ and keep all of God's Word always being quick to repent as Abraham did then we are circumcised in heart and regardless of our race we are grafted into a spiritual Israel of the New Covenant and we ARE the children of Abraham.

Circumcision of the flesh has a fault, which is that those circumcised in the flesh still could not obey their Father in heaven; therefore circumcision of the flesh was replaced by a much better circumcision: A circumcision of the heart through the sacrifice of Christ which atoned for sin, removing the barrier of sin [the foreskin of our heart] which comes between us and God the Father.

The foreskin of our hearts [which is our sins] must be removed!

> **Isaiah 59:1** Behold, the LORD's hand is not shortened, that it cannot save; neither his ear heavy, that it cannot hear: **59:2 But your iniquities have separated between you and your God, and your sins have hid his face from you, that he will not hear.**

As it is written:

> **Deuteronomy 10:16** Circumcise therefore the **foreskin of your heart**, and be no more stiffnecked [stubborn and self-willed].

Our sins are removed by our sincere repentance and our baptismal commitment to go and sin no more through faith in the sacrifice of Jesus Christ the Lamb of God; which then reconciles us to God the Father and makes us the seed of Abraham in a spiritual sense.

It is the circumcision of the heart [the removal of sin by the application of the sacrifice of Christ] which makes us Abraham's seed not the circumcision of the flesh; which does not remove sin nor does it make us truly spiritual sons of Abraham or sons of God our Father in heaven.

Galatians 3:8 And the scripture, foreseeing that God would justify the heathen through faith, preached before the gospel unto Abraham, saying, In thee shall **all nations** be blessed. **3:9** So, then they which be of faith are blessed with faithful Abraham.

Those who repent and turn away from rebellion against God the Father; those who STOP sinning: Will then have the sacrifice of the Lamb of God applied to them!

Our faith in Christ; which must be a living faith of sincere repentance from evil works to become obedient to the whole Word of God the Father, just as Jesus Christ was and is obedient to God the Father: will result in the application of Christ's atoning sacrifice to us: And being justified by that sacrifice we will be reconciled to God the Father in heaven.

> **Romans 2:13 (For not the hearers of the law are just before God, but the doers of the law shall be justified.**
>
> **James 2:14** What doth it profit, my brethren, though a man say he hath faith, and have not works? Can faith save him? **2:5** If a brother or sister be naked, and destitute of daily food, **2:16** and one of you say unto them, Depart in peace, be ye warmed and filled; notwithstanding ye give them not those things which are needful to the body, what doth it profit?
>
> **2:17** Even so **faith, if it hath not works, is dead, being alone. 2:18** Yea, a man may say, You hast faith, and I have works. **Show me thy faith without thy works, and I will show thee my faith by my works. 2:19** Thou believest that there is one God; thou doest well: the devils also believe, and tremble.

The demons believe God yet they will not obey God's Word, therefore their belief brings them nothing but the sure knowledge of their coming judgment.

> **2:20** But wilt thou know, O vain man, that **faith without works is dead**?
>
> **2:21** Was not Abraham our father justified [justified by his deeds] by works when he [obeyed God] had offered Isaac his son upon the

altar? **2:22** Seest thou how faith wrought [worked with] with his works and **by works was faith made perfect**? **2:23** And the scripture was fulfilled which saith, Abraham believed God, and it was imputed unto him for righteousness: and he was called the Friend of God.

2:24 Ye see then how that by works a man is justified, and not by faith only. **2:25** Likewise also was not Rehab the harlot justified by works, when she had received the messengers, and had sent them out another way? **2:26** For **as the body without the spirit is dead, so faith without works is dead.**

Yes, there is a spirit in our body, it is a spirit of man, a spirit in man; and without the body it doesn't function, it doesn't think, it is not conscious.

Our spirit must be plugged into the body and the spirit of man and the body work together. Just so faith must be plugged into works, and works into the faith; so that trust and belief result in the works of faith.

Faith without works cannot stand: If we have faith, if we believe God, we will do what God says; which is our works of faith.

We cannot do what God says if we do not believe [have faith that his Word is true] Him; any more than the spirit can live without the body.

If we have faith and no works, our faith is meaningless: it is a waste of time. Believing without acting on that belief is a waste of time; it won't get us anywhere.

We are only justified by the application of Christ's sacrifice! The unrepentant sinner will NOT have the sacrifice of Christ applied to him or her and will NOT be justified before God until they sincerely repent and commit to STOP sinning!

The true circumcision of the New Covenant is spiritual, of the heart and spirit, and not of the flesh.

Circumcision of the flesh profits nothing spiritually; even baptism and ordination, or attending some corporate church organization profits nothing at all; UNLESS we are circumcised of the heart through sincere repentance from all sin and compromising with any part of the whole Word of God, followed by a commitment to diligently believe and live by every Word of God and only then will the sacrifice of Jesus Christ be applied to us.

If we are baptized, ordained, or attend corporate church services, or are physically circumcised: It means absolutely NOTHING unless we do the deeds of Abraham and have his faith to trust and obey Almighty God!

Circumcision of the flesh was a sign of the Mosaic Covenant and when that Covenant passed away because of its weakness: It was replaced with a New and better Covenant, a spiritual Covenant.

The sign of the New Covenant is the circumcision of the heart: Which is repentance from rebellion and sin, a commitment to obey God the Father and the application of the atoning sacrifice of Christ! This circumcises our hearts by removing all PAST sins and reconciles us to God the Father by removing the barrier of sin that had existed between us and God the Father; which barrier is our rebellion and sin!

This message about circumcision is an explanation of the process of salvation!

Yes, the truly converted Gentiles are grafted into a New Covenant spiritual Israel, being filled with faith in God. They are obedient in faith and are the seed of Abraham, for Abraham believed God and coupled that belief with obedience!

Abraham believed God. Abraham acted on that belief and obeyed God, showing forth the works of his faith. That is true faith!

Faith is not just belief, it is action based on belief. We can believe all we want to and if we do nothing about it, it has done us absolutely no good. We must believe God, and we must act on that belief by doing what God says.

If we believe in the sacrifice of Christ, then we must act to stop sinning so that his sacrifice may then be applied to us! This is called "SINCERE REPENTANCE"!

Galatians 3:10 For as many as are of the works of the law are under a curse: for it is written, Cursed is every one that continues not in all things which are written in the book of the law to do them.

If we do not have faith in the atoning sacrifice of Christ, his perfect sinless life and resurrection, and if we justify breaking God's Word in even the smallest point, we are cursed [facing death] and we must pay the penalty for having broken the Word of God.

There is no remission of PAST sin without sincere repentance from all past sin, a commitment to sin no more in future and the application of the sacrifice of Christ!

The penalty for transgressing the law or any part of the Word of God is death; Adam died for his rebellion against God! And the only way to be saved from being forced to pay the penalty we have earned is to sincerely repent of all PAST sins, resolve to STOP sinning in future, be baptized, and have faith in the promises and the sacrifice of Jesus Christ.

3:11 But that no man is justified by the law in the sight of God, it is evident: for, the just shall live by faith. **3:12** And the law is not of faith: but, the man that does them shall live in them. **3:13** Christ hath redeemed us from the curse of the law, [If we sincerely repent and STOP sinning, Jesus Christ will redeem us from the penalty for having broken the law.] being made a curse for us, having died for us: for it is written, Cursed is every one that hangeth on a tree.

The law itself is not a curse: It is a great blessing. But there is a curse of the law, and the curse of the law is the penalty that must be paid when the law is broken; when the law is broken, the penalty is death.

We can only be saved from that penalty through sincere repentance for not obeying God and then to dedicate ourselves to live by every Word of God from henceforth and forever more.

Then the atoning sacrifice of Jesus Christ will be applied to us; at which point we will be given God's Spirit; and the Spirit of Christ and of God the Father will dwell in us empowering us to live by every Word of God the Father and Jesus Christ.

And if we should slip now and then, or here and there unintentionally; we have faith that Christ's sacrifice will atone for us if we sincerely repent. That does not justify continuing in sin, it does not justify habitual sin; but it is there to save us, when and if we do unintentionally slip.

3:14 That the blessing of Abraham might come also on the Gentiles through Jesus Christ; that we might receive the promise of the Spirit through faith.

The Spirit of God, which empowers us to keep God's Word, which imparts us with the very nature of God; the Holy Spirit is given through our sincere repentance from all past sin and faith in the sacrifice of Christ, and our willingness to obey Christ and God the Father to turn from our sins and to diligently live by every Word of God the Father in future (Mat 4:4).

3:15 Brethren, I speak after the manner of men; Though it be but a man's agreement or covenant, yet if it be confirmed, no man disannuls, or adds to it.

When you have a firm covenant or a contract with somebody, nobody can break it, or disannul it, or change it; without a penalty. It is a commitment made between two people.

3:16 Now, to Abraham and his seed were the promises made. He said not, and to seeds, as of many; but as of one, And to **thy seed, which is Christ**.

The promise of God to Abraham was that through Abraham's seed Isaac, who was a type of Jesus Christ; God would bless all people, which includes ALL races.

3:17 And this I say, that the covenant, that was confirmed before of God in Christ, the law, which was four hundred and thirty years later [The Mosaic Covenant began at Sinai 430 years after the promise was made to Abraham in Ur.], cannot disannul that covenant or that promise that God made to Abraham, that it should make the promise of no effect.

That is, Jesus Christ was God before he was made flesh, and he promised Abraham in Ur: "in your seed shall all flesh be blessed." And the Mosaic Covenant at Sinai coming 430 years after the promise was made in Ur cannot disannul the promise that God made to Abraham.

> As a slight aside here, that is why the descendants of Abraham, that is, the tribes of Israel and Judah are being blessed in this latter day; to fulfill all the promises made by God to the ancients. The Mosaic Covenant ended with the death of the Husband Jesus Christ. However, God's promises have not ended. And he is keeping the promises he made to Abraham, to Isaac, to Jacob, to Joseph and to Moses, that he would bless their descendants. And God is keeping his promise and Abraham's descendants are being blessed at this time.

> Because of the overspreading of our abominations, the blessing [Christ's application of the Daily Sacrifice in heaven, representing the nation under God's blessings and protection which restrains the false abomination of iniquity] will be stopped and we will be corrected.

Until our correction we are now receiving the latter day blessings that were promised to Abraham, to Isaac, to Jacob, and to Joseph.

Back to Galatians and Paul who is writing about the blessing of the coming of Christ and of his atoning sacrifice which was made for not just Jews but for all people of faithful obedience.

The New Covenant of spiritual Israel is for all who would respond to God the Father's call, all who would believe and sincerely repent and turn from sin, dedicating themselves to diligently keep and live by the whole Word of God.

This promise made to Abraham was firm and cannot be altered or changed by subsequent covenants: Therefore, the Mosaic Covenant cannot alter the promise of the spiritual New Covenant, that God made to Abraham concerning the blessing of atonement through his seed; Jesus Christ.

3:18 For if the inheritance be of the law, it is no more of a promise: but God gave it to Abraham by promise.

God's promise to Abraham was a promise and was not part of the Mosaic Covenant and the various laws. It was a personal promise of God to Abraham.

3:19 Wherefore, then, serveth the law? The law was added because of transgressions [or wickedness,] till the seed, [that is, the one seed] should come to whom the promise was made; and it was ordained by angels in the hand of a mediator. **3:20** Now, a mediator is not a mediator of one, but God is one.

That is, a mediator mediates between two parties. A mediator does not deal with just one party. And there is one mediator between God and man, and that is Jesus Christ. He came as our mediator, and our Deliverer, and our Sacrifice. And he mediates between us and God the Father.

No, Mary is not a mediatrix and the saints do not mediate for people, here is no other mediator between God and man, than Jesus Christ.

> **1 Timothy 2:5** For there is one God, and **one mediator between God and men, the man Christ Jesus;**

Galatians 3:21 Is the law then against the promises of God? . . .

Are God's commandments and the Covenants somehow contrary to or against the promises of God? Of course not.

As Paul says, . . . God forbid: for if there had been a law given which could have given life, truly righteousness should have been by the law.

Yet keeping the law does not provide payment for past sin. What provides atonement and forgiveness is our repentance coupled with the application of the actual sacrifice of the Creator.

3:22 But the scripture hath concluded that all are under sin, that the promise of faith of Jesus Christ might be given to them who believe. **3:23** But before faith came, we were kept under [the penalty of having broken the law] law and shut up unto the faith which should afterwards be revealed.

Paul says, until faith came in, and until the sacrifice of Jesus Christ came into the picture, until Christ actually fulfilled his mission; we were all under the curse [that the penalty of breaking the law must be paid] of the law. We were all facing death for having broken the commandments until Christ's sacrifice and faith entered.

Christ's sacrifice was made and he was resurrected to spirit, and we can have faith in that sacrifice and resurrection; faith that Christ lived a sinless life and his sacrifice atoned for our sincerely repented sin and faith that we, if Christ lives in us keeping the whole Word of God in us, can also be resurrected to spirit like he was.

Faith then enters into the picture and the concept of having to die for our PAST sin fades away, as we are justified by our sincere repentance and commitment to STOP sinning, and faith in the atoning sacrifice of Christ which paid the penalty in our place.

3:24 Wherefore the law was our schoolmaster to bring us to Christ, that we might be justified by faith. **3:25** For after faith is come, we are no longer under a schoolmaster.

We needed to learn not to sin and therefore we faced a penalty for our sin; to teach us not to sin.

When we learn not to sin any more and to REPENT of our PAST sin; then FAITH in the atoning sacrifice of Christ enters the picture and delivers the REPENTANT from the need to pay the penalty for PAST sin. This DOES NOT JUSTIFY continuing in sin!

3:26 For you are all the children of God through faith in Christ Jesus. **3:27** For as many of you as have been baptized into Christ have put on Christ.

If we have been called by God and have sincerely repented of all past sins, then Jesus Christ will dwell in us through the power of God's Spirit; empowering us to live as Christ lived, living by every Word of God (Mat 4:4).

3:28 There is neither Jew nor Greek, there is neither bond nor free, there is neither male nor female: for you are all one in Christ Jesus. **3:29** And if you be in Christ, then are ye all Abraham's seed, and heirs according to the promise.

The converted of the New Covenant spiritual Israel are not Mosaic Jews and they are not Gentiles, they are all heirs together of the promise of God.

Those who are faithful are all the children of Abraham and the children of God, because they are sincerely repentant and filled with Abraham's faith and obedience to live by every Word of God in future.

The sign of the New Covenant is not circumcision in the flesh, **it is circumcision of the heart;** which is heartfelt REPENTANCE from sin and going forward to faithfully live by every Word of God, living as Jesus Christ lives!

> **1 John 2:6** He that saith he abideth in him ought himself also so to walk, even as he walked.

The sign of the New Covenant is REPENTANCE, FAITH and the diligent keeping of every Word of God! It is FAITH in Christ, married to the works of REPENTANT OBEDIENCE that saves! It is Faith in Jesus Christ, faith in God the Father, faith in the sacrifice that was applied to blot out our REPENTED sins.

Faith that the Spirit of God is given to us and dwells in us and empowers us to live by every Word of God and empowers us to please God; and fills us with the love of God, which is to live by every Word of God.

We must now live by faith; because before, we were dead in our sins having broken the law and therefore under the penalty of death; and sin is the transgression of the law (1 John 3:4).

Sin is the transgression of the law. We have all broken the law at some point in our lives. Therefore, we are all under the penalty of having broken the law which is death.

It is a stopping of sinning [REPENTANCE] and faith in Jesus Christ and the application of his sacrifice to atone for our past sins; that brings into a proper relationship with God and circumcises our hearts; removing the BARRIER of sin which separates us from Almighty God.

And it is through sincere repentance, a commitment to sin no more and faith in the application of the sacrifice of Christ reconciling us to God; that the Holy Spirit can be given to us; and that Spirit then empowers us to live by every Word of God in the future.

Once a penalty for breaking a law has been paid, that does not in any way justify continuing to break the law.

If you have a habit of going through red lights, and you go and pay a fine, and the next time you are caught, you tell the judge, "Well, I paid the fine last time, I have a right to do it from now on." He is going to laugh at you, and probably take away your license, and maybe give you a few days to cool off in a cell.

The fact is, when we pay a fine, it only pays for PAST law breaking. It does not pay for any future law breaking and that is true with God as well. The sacrifice of Christ applied to us, only atones for sincerely repented PAST law breaking. It does not permit us to indulge ourselves in future law breaking.

If we inadvertently break the law in future, we must repent, and have the sacrifice applied again, or we will face the penalty for that particular act of law breaking.

And there will come a time, that if we willfully break the law and justify ourselves in doing so; that Jesus Christ is going to run out of patience with us.

If we are not sincere, if we are not honest, if we don't really want to live by God's Word; we are not really trying to please God and in time God's patience will end. Christs sacrifice will no longer be applied to us until we straighten up, and wake up, and start really genuinely repenting, and start really genuinely trying to please God.

Sincere repentance, faith and the works of faith save us from the penalty of sin, which is death. It is faith and the sacrifice of Christ which saves us.

That faith does not entitle us to then go out and incur the penalty a second time, and a third, and a fourth, and on and on, and on.

It is faith in the sacrifice married to the works of faith, married to sincere repentance and a dedicated commitment to STOP sinning; which brings atonement for PAST sin, PAST law breaking and allows us to be reconciled with God the Father.

Which atonement for sin then places us into a proper relationship with God and through faith, we are given God's Holy Spirit which will then empower us to live by every Word of God from then on.

Paul continues with his guidance and instruction to the people, trying to reconcile the Jews and the Gentile converts with each other, and to make them realize that they are all part of the same body, and through faith, they are all the children of Abraham.

> **1 Corinthians 7:19 Circumcision** is nothing, and uncircumcision is nothing, but the keeping of the commandments of God. [is everything]

Physical circumcision, baptism and even ordination are absolutely NOTHING; IF we are not zealous to live by every Word of God!

Spiritual circumcision is the removal of the sin that separates us from God and the writing of the whole Word of God on our hearts and in our minds through the Holy Spirit, enabling us to live by every Word of God.

> **Jeremiah 31:33** But this shall be the covenant that I will make with the house of Israel; After those days, saith the Lord, I will put my law in their inward parts, and write it in their hearts; and will be their God, and they shall be my people.

Those who compromise or reject any part of the Word of God, as is commonly done in today's spiritual Ekklesia, will have no part in the New Covenant resurrection to spirit.

Galatians 4

Galatians 4:1 Now, I say, that the heir, as long as he is a child, differs nothing from a servant, though he is the lord of all.

If someone inherits a huge estate but is still a child, they need to mature and learn how to handle that responsibility before that responsibility can be given to them.

4:2 And the child is under tutors and governors until the time appointed of the father. **4:3** Even so we, when we were children, were in bondage under the elements of the world.

We were placed in this physical world so that we could learn obedience to God our Father, and so that we might experience its evils and learn to trust in God and to live with godly wisdom.

4:4 But when the fullness of the time was come, God sent forth his Son, made of a woman, made under the law, **4:5** to redeem them which were under the law, that **we might receive the adoption of sons.**

Jesus Christ became flesh and came under the potential penalty of the law for any possible sin.

Mary herself had at some point in her life committed some sin for sure, as we all have; and she was worthy to die as we all are. Jesus Christ died for her as much as for anybody else. We are all facing the same penalty for breaking the law until we sincerely repent and STOP sinning, and the atoning sacrifice of Christ is applied to us.

It is when we have sincerely repented, and committed and dedicated ourselves to go and sin no more, that the sacrifice of Jesus Christ can be applied to us and we may then receive the gift of the Holy Spirit by which we may overcome all sin so that we might receive the adoption of God as his sons.

4:6 And because you are [adopted] sons, God hath sent forth the Spirit of his Son into your hearts, crying, Abba, Father.

The Spirit of the Son, the Spirit of Jesus Christ; is the Holy Spirit of God. And Jesus Christ said, "I can do nothing of myself, all things I have done by the Father" (John 5:30); And again, he said: "I have kept my Father's commandments" (John 15:10).

And that same Spirit will be given to us and we will be able to cry, Father, Father, with true genuine love and have a real, true, genuine relationship, a father-son relationship with God the Father, through the Spirit of God the Father and Jesus Christ dwelling in us.

We, with the Spirit of God the Father and Jesus Christ dwelling in us; will love God the Father, will obey God the Father and we will please God the Father in Christ-like zeal: And we will have the same kind of relationship with God the Father that Jesus Christ had and has.

If we do not love and keep the whole Word of God with dedicated zeal, then we do not have the Holy Spirit of God; we are of another spirit.

4:7 Wherefore thou art no more a servant, but a son; and if a son, then an heir of God through Christ.

That is, when we have a correct kind of relationship with God the Father and we become sons of the Father, we are also heirs and will receive an inheritance from the Father of eternal life even as Jesus Christ did.

Christ will become King of kings over all the earth; and we will have a part, receiving a portion of that inheritance working with Christ as younger brothers and fellow heirs.

4:8 Howbeit then, when ye knew not God, ye did service unto them which by nature are not gods. **4:9** But now, after that ye have known God, or rather you are known of God, how is it, how can you turn again to the weaker and beggarly elements, whereunto you desire to be in bondage?

I ask as Paul did: If we have been justified by repentance and faith. You who are circumcised in heart with the circumcision of Christ into a New and better Covenant; **why do you want to remain in the sin you were delivered from?**

Why do you compromise with the Word of God and call the Sabbath holy and then openly pollute it, or by becoming lax in any zeal to keep God's Word?

Why would you want to go back into the bondage of sin, again facing the death penalty for sin and law breaking, when you have been liberated from bondage to sin and delivered from a death sentence for our sins through repentance and faith in the atonement of Jesus Christ?

4:10 For you observe days, and months, and times, and years.

This is about various Pharisaic traditions; fasting two or three times a week and doing special things on certain days, and today men even using prayer shawls and wearing skull caps. Paul is referring to traditions of men here; he is not talking about God's commanded Sabbath or God's commanded Holy Days, or the Word of God. He is talking about the traditions of men, as he says. This is also about our non scriptural traditions of men today.

Paul explains about returning to the weak and beggarly elements [worldly man devised religious traditions] of this world, instead of living by every Word of God.

The things of God are not weak and beggarly. They are holy and right and just and good, the law of God is holy.

> **Romans 7:12** Wherefore the law is holy, and the commandment holy, and just, and good.

Why then does anyone seek to turn away from the things of God to go back to these beggarly, weak things? To go back to observing all of these vain traditions and teachings of men, including the tradition of not eating with the Gentiles.

Converted New Covenant, circumcised in heart Gentiles and Jews; who are living by every Word of God; ARE spiritually clean because they have sincerely repented and now live by every Word of God, and they are to remain spiritually clean through living by every Word of God forever more!

Galatians 4:11 I am afraid of you, lest I have bestowed upon you my labors in vain. **4:12** Brethren, I beseech you, be as I am; for I am as you are or as you should be: you have not injured me at all. **4:13** You know how through infirmity of the flesh I preached the gospel unto you at the first. **4:14** And my temptation, which was in my flesh you despised not, nor rejected; but received me as an angel of God, even as Jesus Christ. **4:15** Where is then the blessedness you spake of? For I bear you record, that, if it had been possible, you would have plucked out your own eyes, and have given them to me.

Paul fears for the Galatians, fearing that they have been deceived into following the false traditions of men when they should be exalting the whole Word of God.

Brethren, we have also been diverted from following our Deliverer into following idols of men and many false traditions of men: We follow men away from any zeal to keep the whole Word of God.

From Doctrine to Prophecy, from Calendar to Sabbath and High Days, we follow the false traditions of men and not the Word of God.

4:16 Am I therefore become your enemy, because I tell you the truth?

Paul emphasizes that what he is telling the people is the truth and is for their good, so that all would remember that both sincerely repentant and faithful Jews and Gentiles are the heirs of Abraham.

If we are faithful to follow God as Abraham did: Then we are the children of Abraham, the children of faith and the children of God: And we should not look down on each other or refuse to associate with each other because of race or any other non scriptural issue.

4:17 They zealously affect you, but not well; yea, they would exclude you, that you might affect them. **4:18** But it is good to be zealously affected always in a good thing, and not only when I am present with you. **4:19** My little children, of whom I travail in birth again until Christ be formed in you, **4:20** I desire to be present with you now and to change my voice; for I stand in doubt of you. **4:21** Tell me, you that desire to be under the law [Those who believe that the law disannuls the promises of God should listen to the law.], do you not hear the law?

4:22 Do you not hear the law itself? For it is written, that Abraham had two sons, the one by a bondmaid, the other by a freewoman. **4:23** But he, who was of the bondwoman, was born after the flesh.

This is an allegory. The one who was born of the bondwoman, the servant, was born after the flesh, is a likeness of bondage to the ways of this world.

But he who was born of the free woman was by promise. For God had promised Abraham that his wife Sarah his free will wife would have a son.

4:25 And these things are an allegory: for these are the two covenants; the one from the Mount Sinai, which genders to bondage, which is Agar. **4:26** For this Agar is Mount Sinai in Arabia, and answers to Jerusalem [physical Israel] which now is, and is in bondage with her children. **4:27** But Jerusalem which is above [representing the Spiritual Israel of the New Covenant] is free [from bondage to sin], which is the mother of us all.

Physical Jerusalem is a type of the Mosaic Covenant made at Sinai represented by the son of the bond servant. There is no eternal salvation promised in the Mosaic Covenant and there is no spiritual atonement or forgiveness for sin there. There is no promise of eternal life. There is no promise of the Holy Spirit. There is no promise of any of these things.

The Mosaic Covenant promises that God will bless the people, and that they will be great and wealthy nations; if, and that's a big if, they are faithful to the Mosaic Covenant and obedient to their Husband. The whole book of Deuteronomy is a warning from Moses telling the people that they must obey God to receive the blessings of the Mosaic Covenant. And if they will not obey God, they will eventually see those blessings withdrawn and removed.

The Mosaic Covenant ended because it failed to bring eternal salvation (Jeremiah 31:31). The New Covenant is pictured by the New Jerusalem and the son of the free woman. The New Covenant is a heavenly thing, a divine thing in which the Creator God himself gives his life for his creation.

All those who are called and respond and sincerely repent and who in faith have Christ's sacrifice applied to them; can go forward in faith, to live by every Word of God and to have a relationship as a true son of God the Father; and as a person of faith, a true child of Abraham.

Paul says over and over and over again; that all those who repent and faithfully keep the Word of God, and have the sacrifice of Christ applied to them, are the true spiritually circumcised children of Abraham.

All those who are of the Mosaic Covenant, circumcised in the flesh and not in the spirit, are spiritually under the penalty of sin because they lack faith and do not accept the sacrifice [of Christ] of the spiritual New Covenant of Jeremiah 31:31, that could save them. They can receive physical blessings for faithfulness to the Mosaic Covenant, but they cannot receive the spiritual blessing of the resurrection to eternal life as a spirit.

There is no effective atonement for spiritual sin in the Mosaic Covenant because the death of lambs, goats, doves and cattle could only keep one in good standing in the Mosaic Covenant, and could not truly atone for sin on the spiritual level of the New Covenant with its promise of eternal life; because the life of an animal is of much less value than any person.

In due time because of its weakness in lacking spiritual atonement and promises (Jer 31) the Mosaic Covenant ended with the death of the Husband, so there is no covenant anymore of the Mosaic type.

Atonement for sin is all about REPENTANCE and FAITH in God's promise that the death of Messiah would truly atone for all sincerely repented sin.

Today there is only the New Covenant, and those who lack faith, regardless of whether they call themselves Jews, Christians, the Church of God, Hindus or whatever, if they lack faith in Christ to sincerely repent of PAST sins and to sin no more, going onward to live as Christ lived; then the atonement of Jesus Christ, the sacrifice of Christ cannot be applied to them. Therefore, their law breaking cannot be atoned for until they sincerely repent.

4:28 For it is written, rejoice, thou barren that bears not; break forth and cry, thou that travails not: for the desolate hath many more children than she which hath an husband. Now, we, brethren, as Isaac was, are the children of promise. **4:29** But as then he that was born after the flesh. And he who was born, [that is, Ishmael] after the flesh, persecuted him that was born after the Spirit or after the promise,

Ishmael being a slave persecuted Isaac the free man, in an allegory that those enslaved to sin will persecute the person freed from sin.

Ishmael born of a slave after the carnal manner - Abraham consorting with a slave - which was a matter of men trying to solve their own problems by their own means [ways] and NOT trusting God to keep his own promises; in this case instigated by Sarah.

Ishmael was by man's efforts, man trying to attain God's promises by his own ways; while Isaac was by faith in God's power and will to keep his promises.

4:30 Nevertheless what saith the scripture? [it says,] cast out the bondwoman and her son: for the son of the bondwoman shall not be an heir with the son of the freewoman. **4:31** So, then, brethren, we are not children of the bondwoman, but of the free.

Ishmael and Isaac are here used to demonstrate the difference between works without faith [the Mosaic Covenant]; and works by faith [the New Covenant].

Abraham should have demonstrated his faith by believing God and waiting patiently [while doing the works of FAITH for God to keep his promise concerning a son. Yet, this connection to Hagar was allowed and blessed with a son as an instructional allegory.

We are heirs together with Jesus Christ by faith in the atoning sacrifice of Christ: Faith in the power of God's Spirit and faith in the power of God the Father to resurrect his children to eternal life as he resurrected Jesus Christ to spirit and eternal life.

We will only have a good relationship with God and will only be filled with his Spirit, if we are living by every Word of God which is the righteous works of faith; and then we can call God our Father and he will call us his sons.

Then if we remain faithful to continue to live by every Word of God we will receive a reward of eternal life and an inheritance; for the law commands that we obey our fathers!

Galatians 5

Galatians 5:1 Stand fast therefore in the liberty wherewith Christ hath made us free, [yes his sacrifice has made us free from bondage to sin and free from having to pay the penalty of death] and be not entangled again with the yoke of bondage, [bondage to sin].

Once we are liberated from the penalty of sin, from the penalty for breaking the Word of God; through our repentance and our faith in Christ and his sacrifice we should stop sinning and not come into bondage to sin again. We should not continue in sin. We should rather turn our backs on sin and start living by every Word of God.

5:2 Behold, I, Paul, say unto you, that if ye be circumcised [in the flesh only and not in the spirit, having a cutting in the flesh while continuing in sin], Christ shall profit you nothing.

If you insist on circumcision in the flesh instead of circumcision of the spirit [heart (Deu 10:16, Jer 4:4)], you can have no part in the New Covenant: which is a circumcision of the heart, a sincere repentance and a passionate dedication to "go and sin no more," coupled with faith in the atoning sacrifice of Jesus Christ.

We are to be part of a New and better Covenant as promised in Jeremiah 31!

Jeremiah 31:31 Behold, the days come, saith the LORD, that I will make a new covenant with the house of Israel, and with the house of Judah:

31:32 Not according to the covenant that I made with their fathers in the day that I took them by the hand to bring them out of the land of Egypt; which my covenant they brake, although **I was an husband unto them**, saith the LORD:

31:33 But this shall be the covenant that I will make with the house of Israel; After those days, saith the LORD, **I will put my law in their inward parts, and write it in their hearts; and will be their God, and they shall be my people.**

This New Covenant circumcision of heart reconciles people to God:

Deuteronomy 30:6 And the Lord thy God will circumcise thine heart, and the heart of thy seed, to love the Lord thy God with all thine heart, and with all thy soul, that thou mayest live.

Jeremiah 31:34 And they shall teach no more every man his neighbour, and every man his brother, saying, Know the LORD: for they shall all know me, from the least of them unto the greatest of them, saith the LORD: for I will forgive their iniquity, and I will remember their sin no more.

Physical circumcision is nothing if we do not keep God's Word; we need the spiritual circumcision of heart to remove the barrier of sin which separates us from God and enables us to live by every Word of God, which brings eternal life.

It is sincere repentance from sin and faith in the sacrifice of Christ to atone for repented PAST sins, and then to go forward living by every Word of God, which saves us.

Galatians 5:3 For I testify again to every man that is [becomes] circumcised [in the flesh only and is not circumcised in the [heart] spirit], that he is a debtor to do the whole law [Meaning that he will still be required to pay the penalty for having broken the law, since he has no redemption from past sins]. The convert who is circumcised in the flesh only, is joining the Mosaic Covenant and not the spiritual New Covenant of circumcision of the heart.

A convert must have his PAST sins removed by a circumcision of the heart through sincere repentance and faith in Christ's atoning sacrifice; which alone can redeem him from sin and reconcile him to God the Father.

We can ONLY enter the New Covenant and be reconciled to God by a circumcision of the heart - through the removal of the sins that separate us from God - by sincere repentance from sin, and by faith and acceptance of the sacrifice of Jesus Christ with a whole hearted commitment to live by every Word of God in future.

Jesus Christ is become of no effect to those who try to justify themselves by law keeping; because FUTURE law keeping cannot atone for PAST sins.

There is the key. You cannot be justified for PAST sins by future law keeping.

We are justified through grace which is the pardon that God gives to us because of our sincere repentance, after which the sacrifice of Jesus Christ is applied to us paying the penalty of death for us

Therefore when we STOP sinning, God the Father pardons us: He reaches out and gives us grace or pardon and we are justified by the application of the sacrifice of the Lamb of God.

We cannot be justified by perfectly keeping a law [in future] which we have already broken in the PAST: To be justified requires the application of the sacrifice of the Lamb of God for all sincerely repented past sins, which must be followed by a diligent commitment to "go and sin no more" in future. In worldly terms if we murder and then never murder again, we are still murderers and the penalty must still by payed in spite of our subsequent obedience.

5:4 Christ is become of no effect unto you, whoever of you [thinks that you] are justified by the law; you have fallen from grace. **5:5** For we through the Spirit wait for the hope of righteousness by faith. **5:6** For in Jesus Christ neither circumcision avails anything, nor uncircumcision; but faith which works by love.

Once we have sinned, physical circumcision, baptism or ordination means nothing until the penalty which we have earned is paid; either by us or by our Redeemer through the application of his sacrifice to the sincerely repentant.

5:7 You did run well; who did hinder you that you should not obey the truth? **5:8** This persuasion comes not of him that called you.

They were not persuaded by God, or by Christ, that the Mosaic Covenant circumcision of adult converts who were already circumcised in heart. was required to enter the New Covenant. They were persuaded of this by men who wanted to force them to submit to their own ideas.

No, we need to be circumcised in heart, in the spirit; and have that covering, that veil of sin which comes between us and God: Removed!

Physical circumcision is the removal of a piece of skin, which acts a veil or a covering and spiritual circumcision is the removal of the veil of sin which separates us from God.

In the New Covenant, spiritual circumcision is the removal of the veil of sin which separates us from God, and which is removed by sincere repentance, a baptismal commitment to sin no more and the application of the sacrifice of Christ. That is, spiritual New Covenant circumcision is the effectual removal of the sin which separates us from God the Father.

Spiritual circumcision is the removal of that veil or barrier of sin that comes between us and God the Father; and that can be done only through sincere repentance, a dedicated commitment to sin no more, and faith in the sacrifice of Christ.

We cannot be justified from PAST sin by cutting off a piece of skin from off our bodies. We must have the sin removed; and sin is the transgression of the law. Therefore, when Christ's sacrifice is applied to us and that barrier, that veil of sin is removed, we must make sure it STAYS REMOVED by stopping our sinning.

The fleshly piece of skin is a symbol of sin which makes us insensitive to godliness, and removing it is a symbol of removing sin and sensitizes us to the spiritual things of God: The application of the sacrifice of Christ is the TRUE circumcision of the New Covenant; which is the REALITY that removes the sin that comes between us and God.

We must not sin anymore, because if we sin again, that wall, that veil, that covering which separates us from God the Father; goes right back up again, and separates us from God once again.

We need to make sure that that veil, that wall of sin that separates us from God; which is removed upon sincere repentance, a commitment to stop sinning and the application of the sacrifice of Christ is demolished; and that the barrier of sin is NOT to be built up again, once again separating us from God, by our continuing in sin.

5:9 A little leaven leavens the whole lump.

Meaning, as it says in James 2:10, that when you break the law in one point, you have broken the whole law. The whole point here is that a little bit of something which is wrong, or a false teaching; pollutes the whole person. Even a small sin pollutes us and separates us from God.

We must NEVER compromise with God's Word and we must always be quick to repent when we learn that we are in error; in that way, we will grow into the very children of the Most High! We shall become like HIM!

5:10 I have, confidence in you through the Eternal, that you will be none otherwise minded: but he that troubled you shall bear his judgment, whosoever he is. **5:11** And I, brethren, if I yet preach circumcision, why do I yet suffer persecution? Then is the offence of the cross ceased. **5:12** I would they were even cut off which trouble you.

Paul points out that he does not preach a need for physical circumcision of adult converts who have already been spiritually circumcised in the heart; which is why he is persecuted by those who do demand physical circumcision of adult converts, who have already been circumcised in heart.

Paul then says that these others are making this demand because they want to avoid persecution from the larger Jewish community themselves. They are making this demand out of fear of other men.

5:13 For, brethren, you have been called unto liberty [Made free from the bondage of sin and released from the penalty for breaking the law, which is sin.]; only use not liberty for an occasion to the flesh or an occasion to sin [We have been freed from the penalty for PAST sins, and that deliverance is not to be used as an excuse to continue in sin.], but by love serve one another. **5:14** For all the law is fulfilled in one thing; Thou shalt love thy neighbor as thyself. **5:15** But if you bite and devour one another, take heed that ye be not consumed of one another.

If we are continually competing for the preeminence with one another, that's wrong. There is no love in that. Take heed lest we destroy one another or consume one another.

5:16 This I say then, walk in the Spirit, and you shall not fulfill the lust of the flesh.

If we walk in the Spirit of God, we are not going to be divided against God. We are not going to fulfill the lusts of the flesh. We are not going to continue in sin.

5:17 For the flesh lust against the Spirit, and the Spirit against the flesh: and these are contrary the one to the other: so that you cannot do the things that you would.

The spiritual things of God are contrary to the things of the flesh and the things of this world.

5:18 But if you are led of the Spirit [God's Spirit will lead us to sincerely repent of all PAST sin.], you are not under the [death penalty of] law.

Those who have been given God's Spirit receive it because we have sincerely repented and committed to "go and sin no more" and the sacrifice of Jesus Christ the Lamb of God has been applied to us redeeming us from all sincerely repented past sin; therefore we are no longer facing the penalty for having broken the law in the PAST. Then God's Spirit will lead us to keep God's Word in Future.

Any spirit which compromises with any part of God's Word or tolerates any sin is not of God, it is NOT God's Holy Spirit but the spirit of Antichrist!

5:19 Now, the works of the flesh are manifest, which are these: adultery, fornication, uncleanness, lasciviousness [Strong's 766 shameless unbridled lust], **5:20** idolatry, witchcraft, hatred, variance, emulations [Strong's 2205, eager to sin], wrath, strife, seditions, heresies, **5:21** envyings, murders, drunkenness, revellings [Strong's 2970 debauchery, partying with drunkenness and sexual immorality], and such like: of the which I tell you before, as I have also told you in time past, that they which do such things shall not inherit the kingdom of God.

Consider that all these things also have their spiritual equivalent as well as the physical actions, and those who do such things ether physically or spiritually will not be among the first fruits and will not be in the resurrection to spirit; they shall not receive eternal life and will not inherit the Kingdom of God.

Go back over these, and read these things, and do some meditation about envying, and emulation [acting like wicked men], and wrath, and strife, and heresies, sedition, and idolatry, and witchcraft [which is rebellion against living by every Word of God].

Think about these things. Look them up, define them and make that a good personal Bible Study, because these are the things [in either the physical or the spiritual context] that will keep you out of God's kingdom.

These things are the heart and core of the lusts of the flesh which leads to law breaking. Breaking any part of the whole Word of God is sin, but sin always starts with a thought, an idea, a concept, a lust.

Give it some consideration and do some serious study, because these things will keep you out of the resurrection to eternal life.

5:22 But the fruit of the Spirit is love, joy, peace, longsuffering, gentleness, goodness, faith, **5:23** meekness, temperance: against such there is no law. **5:24** And they that are Christ's have crucified the flesh with the affections and lusts thereof.

5:25 If we [expect to live forever through the resurrection to spirit] live in the Spirit, let us also walk in the Spirit [If we are a spiritual people we will conduct ourselves in spiritual manner, living by every Word of God.] **5:26** Let us not be desirous of vain glory provoking one another envying one another.

Galatians 6

Galatians 6:1 Brethren, if a man be overtaken in a fault, ye which are spiritual or spiritually minded, restore such a one in the spirit of meekness; considering yourself, lest you also be tempted. **6:2** Bear ye one another's burdens, and so fulfill the law of Christ.

This work is about warning our dearly beloved brethren to turn back to a passionate zeal to live by EVERY WORD of GOD. Paul and Jesus commanded us to warn our brethren when we see them departing from godliness as the law also commands.

God holds us responsible for rebuking sin, indeed the law of God likens failure to rebuke those who sin as being the same as hating them, because not warning them amounts to allowing them to fall to their destruction.

> **Leviticus 19:17** Thou shalt not hate thy brother in thine heart: thou shalt in any wise rebuke thy neighbour, and not suffer sin upon him.
>
> **Ezekiel 33:2** Son of man, speak to the children of thy people, and say unto them, When I bring the sword upon a land, if the people of the land take a man of their coasts, and set him for their watchman: **33:3** if when he seeth the sword come upon the land, he blow the trumpet, and warn the people; **33:4** then whosoever heareth the sound of the trumpet, and taketh not warning; if the sword come, and take him away, his blood shall be upon his own head. **33:5** He

heard the sound of the trumpet, and took not warning; his blood shall be upon him. But he that taketh warning shall deliver his soul. **33:6** But if the watchman see the sword come, and blow not the trumpet, and the people be not warned; if the sword come, and take any person from among them, he is taken away in his iniquity; but his blood will I require at the watchman's hand.

Galatians 6:3 For if a man think himself to be something, when he is nothing, he is deceiving himself. **6:4** But let every man prove his own work, and then shall he have rejoicing in himself alone, and not in another. **6:5** For every man shall bear his own burden.

Many have falsely claimed that they are apostles or prophets or some such thing. The claims of every man will be revealed in their fruits (Matthew 7) whether they are true or not; and the deeds of every person will be judged by every Word of God.

6:6 Let him that is taught in the word communicate unto him that teaches [the other teachers] in all good things. **6:7** Be not deceived; God is not mocked: for whatsoever a man sows, that shall he reap. **6:8** For he that sows to his flesh, [those who seek physical things and the lusts of the flesh and break the Word of God] shall of the flesh reap corruption [and correction from God]; but he that sows [by living a spiritual life of godliness] to the Spirit shall of the Spirit reap life everlasting.

6:9 And let us not be weary in well doing: for in due season we shall reap, if we faint not. **6:10** As we have therefore opportunity, let us do good unto all men, especially unto them who are of the household of faith.

It is doing good and obeying God to warn our brethren that they have been misled and have fallen away. Even though they might resent the warnings for a short time, we warn them in the hope that they might be saved.

6:11 You see how large a letter I have written unto you with mine own hand. **6:12** As many as desire to make a fair show in the flesh, they constrain you to be circumcised [Certain people required adult converts to be circumcised in the flesh in order to avoid difficulties with the Mosaic Jews.]; only **lest they should suffer persecution** for the cross of Christ. **For neither they themselves who are circumcised keep the law.**

Paul gets to the meat of why some were forcing the adult Gentile converts to be circumcised in the flesh to be considered converted. It was because they were afraid of the Mosaic Jews. They were afraid that if they consorted with Gentiles then the whole Mosaic community would reject them. They wanted to make a show of physical things; so that they could have the pretense of doing things in the Christian, Christ like way, but still be accepted by the Pharisees!

Just like most of today's Ekklesia they wanted to be as inoffensive to this world as possible while still having a pretense of conversion; To appear as much like the mainstream as possible to avoid offending them and to be respected in the mainstream religious community.

The Pharisees were hypocrites, being themselves circumcised on the eighth day, but not keeping the law themselves doing all kinds of sins. You can read that in the Gospels in the words of Christ. They did a lot of things that were not right, but they were physically circumcised and they were proud of that circumcision, and they were zealous for their own traditions and had no zeal for the Word of God, just like today's Ekklesia.

> **Matthew 15:7** Ye hypocrites, well did Esaias prophesy of you, saying, **15:8** This people draweth nigh unto me with their mouth, and honoureth me with their lips; but their heart is far from me. **15:9** But in vain they do worship me, teaching for doctrines the commandments of men.

It is the same today as people say: "We are a part of GOD'S CHURCH" as they then seek to be as worldly as possible, compromising with God's Word and following their own traditions instead of living by God's Word!

Galatians 6:13 For **neither they themselves who are circumcised keep the law**; but desire to have you circumcised, that they may glory in your flesh.

That is, these people don't keep God's Word themselves but they are trying to force others to be circumcised in the flesh so they can claim, "oh look at the converts I made and look at how righteous I am because I got these people to agree with me and MY traditions."

This is just like today's Ekklesia who seek followers after themselves and their own traditions, rather than working to call people to a genuine zeal to live by every Word of God.

6:14 But God forbid that I should glory, save in the cross [sacrifice and resurrection] of our Lord Jesus Christ, by whom the world is crucified unto me, and I unto the world.

Those in the New Covenant are to glory in the fact that they have nothing to do with sin, the old sinful person being dead to sin through sincere repentance, a commitment to sin no more and the application of the sacrifice of Jesus Christ, being made alive in the godliness of living every Word of God

6:15 For in Christ Jesus neither [physical] circumcision [or even baptism] avails anything, nor [physical] uncircumcision [or even baptism], but a new person [spiritually circumcised in heart and changed from the old sinful self to become a new godly person].

6:16 And as many as walk according to this rule [Those that live according to the New Covenant and its spiritual circumcision of the heart, to sincerely repent and have all PAST sin removed by the application of the sacrifice of Jesus Christ and then to go on to live by every Word of God from the heart in future receive a blessing of reconciliation and peace with God.], peace be on them, and mercy, and upon the Israel of God.

6:17 From henceforth let no man trouble me: for I bear in my body the marks of the Lord Jesus. **6:18** Brethren, the grace of our Lord Jesus Christ be with your spirit. Amen.

The whole subject of Galatians is about true conversion and certain Pharisees infiltrating the faithful and wanting to make a show in the flesh that they would not associate with Gentiles unless those Gentiles were circumcised in the flesh.

Paul says over, and over, and over again; that people are justified from PAST sins by sincere repentance and FAITH in the atoning sacrifice of the Lamb of God.

Sin is atoned for through sincere repentance, a baptismal commitment to sin no more and faith in the sacrifice of Christ, and we are to go forward from there, living in a spiritual manner by keeping the whole Word of God in Christ-like zeal through the indwelling of God's Spirit!

We must stop sinning, and sincerely repent, turning away from sin. But the only atonement that exists for PAST sin, is the sacrifice of Christ and our faith in that sacrifice.

All people of faith who have sincerely repented and resolved to sin no more, and have had their sins atoned for through the application of the sacrifice of Christ; are the spiritual children of Abraham and the children of God; circumcised in heart!

Those who are sincerely repentant and follow God in faith need to put God first and then associate with like minded brethren.

We should never look down our noses on somebody in the faith because they are of a different race or because they have minor non scriptural differences.

This idea that some group of people doesn't want to associate with another part of the brotherhood because of race, culture or non scriptural issues is wrong. It is not godly love, it is not loyalty to the household of faith and it is not consistent with the Word of God. Therefore, it is sin.

All those who have repented of sin and been reconciled to God the Father, who work just as hard as they can with the help of God's indwelling Spirit to live by every Word of God our Father with deep passionate love and zeal: Are sons of the SAME FATHER and spiritual brethren!

The book of Galatians is about faith, about justification from sin through the sacrifice of Christ, about turning AWAY from commandment breaking and about refusing to build again the sinful conduct of the past: and it is about brotherly love, and loyalty, and not being afraid of persecutions.

Galatians is about the difference between the Mosaic Covenant of the purely temporary physical; and the spiritual and permanent New Covenant of justification through sincere repentance, commitment to sin no more and faith in the application of the sacrifice of Jesus Christ.

Galatians is about the New Covenant which circumcises the heart and reconciles the sincerely repentant to God for all Eternity; as long as we continually work diligently to root all sin out of our lives.

Let us not turn our backs on God the Father and Jesus Christ to exalt any man or corporate religion as our ultimate moral authority; rather let us exalt God the Eternal Father as Jesus Christ did.

> **Matthew 4:10 Then saith Jesus unto him, Get thee hence, Satan: for it is written, Thou shalt worship the Lord thy God, and him only shalt thou serve.**

The Book of Galatians is about LOVE FOR ALMIGHTY GOD AND THE BRETHREN: A LOVE BORN OF FAITH AND TRUST IN GOD!!!

NOTE: It is not necessary for those already circumcised in heart to be circumcised in the flesh; however our sons are not born circumcised in heart and we must obey God's command to circumcise our sons in the flesh on the eighth day. This is a matter of our obedience to God's command and is a prophetic symbol of their future circumcision of heart.

Ephesians

Ephesians 1

Ephesians 1:1 Paul, an apostle of Jesus Christ by the will of God, to the saints which are at Ephesus and to the faithful in Christ Jesus. **1:2** Grace be to you and peace from God, our Father, and from the Lord Jesus Christ. **1:3** Blessed be the God and Father of our Lord Jesus Christ, who hath blessed us with all spiritual blessings in heavenly places in Christ. **1:4** According as He hath chosen [God had decided from the very beginning to call some before others.] us in Him before the foundation of the world, **that we should be holy and without blame before Him in love.**

God had determined a plan before the world began, planning to call out a certain number ahead of the main harvest of lives as his first fruits.

The called out of God were to be perfected in this world through sincere repentance, the application of the sacrifice of Christ and the gift of the Holy Spirit so that they would become perfect and blameless just as God the Father and Jesus Christ are holy and blameless; perfecting them through a lifetime of faithfully internalizing the very nature of God through a diligent learning, overcoming and keeping of the whole Word of God!

When we have sincerely repented and after our baptismal commitment to sin no more, the application of the sacrifice of Christ the Lamb of God justifies us from our PAST sins and then we can be given the gift of the Holy Spirit, which reconciles us to God the Father, bringing us into a Father son relationship with God.

1:5 Having predestined us unto **the adoption of children** [adoption by God the Father through the atonement of Jesus Christ] by Jesus Christ to himself according to the good pleasure of His will.

God the Father and the one who became Jesus Christ determined before the very creation (2 Ti 1:9, Titus 1:2), that they would be calling out individuals to become the first fruits of the New Covenant; and at an appointed time, there would be a resurrection of all of those first fruits who would then help to bring in the rest of mankind who would also be called into the Family of God.

The plan of God was carefully set up before the foundation of the world. Before the creation of anything, God started out with a plan.

Part of that plan was that through sincere repentance and the sacrifice of Christ the Implementing Creator, sin could be atoned for. That is why Jesus Christ is called the Lamb of God, slain from the foundation of the world (Rev 13:8); because it was before the very foundations of the world that this was all planned out .

1:6: The praise of the glory of His Grace [properly MERCY], wherein He, hath made us accepted in the beloved.

God the Father has made us acceptable to him by calling us to sincere repentance and applying the sacrifice and resurrection of his Beloved Son to the faithful overcomers.

1:7 In whom, [Jesus Christ has redeemed us from sin through the gift of his own life.], we have redemption through His blood, [His sacrifice]. And the forgiveness of sins according to the richness of His Grace; [His mercy -- His compassion on us and on all humanity].

The wisdom of God is spiritual and is beyond the understanding of men; which wisdom he has made known to his faithful called out who are passionately diligent, hungering and thirsting to learn and to live by every Word of God.

1:8 Wherein He hath abounded toward us in all wisdom and prudence, **1:9** having made known unto us the mystery of His will according to His good pleasure; which He hath proposed in Himself.

God has proposed through his plan to gather all things unto himself through Christ, including the salvation of all the races of humanity.

1:10 **That in the dispensation of the fullness of times, He might gather together in one, all things in Christ which are in heaven and which are on the earth even in Christ.**

The called out who are passionately faithful to follow Almighty God and every Word of God in letter and in spirit; will receive an inheritance of eternal life with God the Father and Jesus Christ.

1:11 In whom, also, we have obtained an inheritance.

God predestined to call out a kind of first fruits and set them as a light of godliness shining brightly as an example for all others (Mat 5). Today our light of godly example has grown dim and is flickering out.

1:12 Being predestined, according to the purpose of Him, who worked all things after the council of His own will, that we should be to the praise of His glory who first trusted in Christ.

This does not mean a specific individual was predestined; rather it is referring to the fact that it was predestined, according to the plan; that some would be called early as first fruits.

However, it is also a fact that many are called (Mat 13), and in the end; few will overcome and be chosen. Many are called and few are chosen.

Matthew 22:14 For many are called, but few are chosen.

Ephesians 1:13 In whom ye [the true called out] also trusted, after that ye heard the word of truth, the gospel of your salvation: in whom also after that ye believed, ye **were sealed with that holy Spirit** of promise, **1:14** Which is the earnest of our inheritance until the redemption of the purchased possession, unto the praise of his glory.

Once the Father calls us and we respond to that call sincerely repenting and committing to sin no more, the sacrifice of Jesus Christ is applied to us.

From that point on, we are given the Holy Spirit of God [which is the SEAL (Eph 1:13, 4:30) that we belong to God] to empower us to build a new person in Christ and in God the Father, and to put aside and get rid of and totally destroy that old sinful person.

Here the Holy Spirit is spoken of as something by which we are sealed. This is referred to in the book of Revelation where the 144,000 are sealed.

This is referring to the Holy Spirit of promise, and the sincerely repentant will be sealed with the Holy Spirit.

The Holy Spirit which the dedicated faithful have been given; is only an earnest, a small amount which was given as a small beginning, which we must use and follow towards our full entry into the family of God.

To reach our goal we must then diligently study the whole Word of God and follow God's Spirit to learn all the truth of God [God's Word is Truth] and to keep it. We are to endure and to continually grow and overcome, rejecting error and embracing truth throughout our lives, and that first down payment of the Spirit will grow being exercised by use in us!

1:15 Wherefore, I also, after I heard of your faith in the Lord Jesus, and love unto all the saints, **1:16** cease not to give thanks for you. Making mention of you in my prayers. **1:17** That the God of our Lord Jesus Christ, the Father of glory, may give unto you the spirit of wisdom and revelation in the knowledge of Him.

Let us like Paul give thanks and pray for the faithful, who diligently learn and keep the whole Word of God with dedication and passionate love for all the things of our Father in heaven; that all might overcome and be accounted worthy of the great honor of the resurrection to spirit. Let us also pray for the spiritually lax that a zeal might be ignited for godliness in them.

1:18 The eyes of your understanding being enlightened; that ye may know what is the hope of his calling, and what the riches of the glory of his inheritance in the saints, **1:19** And what is the exceeding greatness of his power to us-ward who believe, according to the working of his mighty power, **1:20** Which he wrought in Christ, when he raised him from the dead, and set him at his own right hand in the heavenly places,

Paul prays that God would pour out his Spirit upon these people, and that the eyes of understanding would be opened, so that we might know the hope of God's calling and the riches of the glorious inheritance of the saints.

Paul reminds the Ephesians that just as God the Father had the power to raise up Jesus Christ to eternal spirit life: God the Father has the power to do the same thing for us.

Jesus Christ was a pioneer. He went through the process first so that we could know that it can be done. We can trust in the Father's power to keep his Word and fulfill his promises!

1:21 Far above all principalities and power and might and dominion and every name that is named, not only in this world, but also, in that which is to come, [God's power is far greater than all the power of all nations and peoples; today, in the past and in the future.] **1:22** And hath put all things under His feet, [under the feet of Christ] and gave him to be the head over all things in the Church, **1:23** which is His body. The fullness of Him that fills all in all.

The true church [the spiritual Ekklesia] is not any corporate assembly of men, it is the body of Christ; it is those who have the seal [the Spirit] of GOD, and follow the Lamb withersoever he goeth. It is not any corporate organization. It is those people in whom the Spirit of God dwells.

Jesus Christ is the head of the spiritual Ekklesia and the true faithful know their head and they obey their head; not going aside after idols of men and false teachings. They obey God the Father in Christ-like zeal, just as Jesus Christ also obeys God the Father.

God's faithful obey God the Father and Jesus Christ by the power of the Holy Spirit, as given by God the Father: For Christ and God the Father are united as one.

As the leg does what the head tells it to, and the arm and the foot obey the head; even so, the various members of the spiritual body do what Jesus Christ tells us to do. We live by every Word of God. We do not follow any person contrary to any part of the Word of God, which is the sins of idolatry and spiritual adultery. We are to follow men ONLY as they follow Jesus Christ and God the Father!

God IS OUR FOUNDATION! If we are truly the people of God!

We look to God FIRST, and we take the things that men tell us and we weigh them in the balance, to see if they are consistent with God's Word or not.

We test the words of men against the standard of God's Word. If the words of men are consistent with the Word of God then we accept those words. If the words of men are not consistent with the Word of God, we are to reject such false words of men.

No man is to be our moral standard! God's Word is to be our standard! We must test the words of all men against God's Word, and hold fast only those things that are consistent with the whole Word of God (1 Thess 5:21)

God's Word is the standard by which all people will be judged!

Jesus Christ and God the Father are the HEAD of the body: not some man! If any man teaches contrary to the HEAD he is not a part of the body. Consider if the foot say to the body: "Follow me contrary to the head," will that body function properly? Should the other body parts follow the foot [any man] instead of the head [God the Father and Jesus Christ]?

By all means, test everything that you hear, and judge them against the whole Word of God regardless of who is saying those words or what title they may claim; and learn to discern between the holy and the profane, being aware of the twisting's that are used to deceive.

Do not be a respecter of persons, be a respecter of God and his Christ. Put God the Father and Jesus Christ [Hebrew: Yeshua Mashiach] first in all things.

Ephesians 2

Ephesians 2:1 And you hath he quickened [given life], who were dead in trespasses and sin.

We were dead, or as good as dead, because we were full of sin and the wages of sin is death. The ultimate result of sin is death. We were as good as dead facing ultimate death for our sins.

> **Romans 6:23** For **the wages of sin is death; but the gift of God is eternal life through Jesus Christ our Lord.**

But, God, by calling us away from sin unto sincere repentance, and a commitment by us to sin no more, and then applying the reconciling sacrifice of the Lamb of God for our PAST sin, has made us alive in faith and the promise of eternal life; if we endure and overcome to the end of our lives.

Once the sacrifice of Christ has been applied to us we no longer face the penalty of death for our PAST sin.

If we persevere and overcome sin by the strength of Jesus Christ living is us we now have the hope of life eternal with God the Father and with Christ, through the sacrifice of Christ and the forgiveness of God the Father.

When we have this hope of life, why would we then turn back to the sin which will result in our death?

Why would we choose to die spiritually? Why do we choose death, when we have been given the hope of eternal life as a spirit?

We must not build again that evil thing which we have destroyed by our sincere repentance and baptismal commitment to stop sinning! We must not return to the bondage to sin and death which Christ delivered us out of by his sacrifice; we must build a new person free from sin and free from those things which result in bondage to sin and ultimately to death!

Ephesians 2:2 When in time past you walked according to the course of this world. According to the prince of the power of the air, the spirit [of Satan] now works in the children of disobedience.

All of us were full of rebellion and sin against God and we walked according to the rebellious works of Satan; following Satan's example in rebelling against living by every Word of God.

2:3 Among whom, also, we all had our conduct, in times past, [living in the lust of our flesh, fulfilling the unlawful desires of flesh and of the mind.] And, were by nature the children of [deserving of God's anger and the wages of sin which is death] wrath even as others.

In other words, we, by being rebellious against God and fulfilling the lusts of our flesh and our imaginations, were worthy of the wrath of God. We were earning God's judgment and correction; we had earned the wages of sin which is death.

2:4 But, God, who is rich in mercy, for His great love – for he loved us, **2:5** even when we were dead in sins.hath quickened us together with Christ, (by grace ye are saved;) **2:6** And hath raised us up together, and **made us sit together in heavenly places in Christ Jesus**:

The dead who were faithful and zealous through Jesus Christ living in them, will awaken and rise up to God in heaven (Rev 15, 19); they shall be changed to spirit and rise with the dead into heaven for the Wedding Feast of the Lamb (Eph 2:6). After which they shall return to rule the earth with Messiah the Christ their collective Husband (Rev 15, 19)!

2:7 That in the ages to come he might shew the exceeding riches of his grace in his kindness toward us through Christ Jesus.

No amount of future law keeping can atone for our PAST sin, therefore God the Father in his awesome mercy sent the Being who gave up his God-hood to become the Son, to die for his creation, so that we might be saved from our repented PAST sins.

That mercy for PAST sins in no way justifies remaining in or going back into sin, like Israel desired to go back into bondage in Egypt.

We are to overcome and grow in the knowledge and nature of God the Father and of the Son; adding to faith the works of faith, just as Abraham and Jesus Christ did; and if we remain faithful to go and sin no more, we will be raised up to spirit and eternal life, as Jesus was raised up to spirit and eternal life!

2:8 For by grace are ye saved through faith; and that not of yourselves: it is the gift of God: **2:9** Not of works, lest any man should boast. **2:10** For we are his workmanship, **created in Christ Jesus unto good works** [We were created to do the good works of living by every Word of God.], **which God hath before ordained that we should walk in them** [God wants us to live by every Word of God performing the good works of faithful godliness.].

In the past we were full of sins and we deserved to die, but God has quickened us [removed the death penalty for our PAST sins and made us spiritually alive] together with Christ; for by grace ye are saved. That is, by God's gift of the sacrifice of the Lamb of God and forgiveness, we are saved.

For God the Father gave his own begotten Son for us and we have the potential to enter into the Family of God, to be resurrected and changed to spirit and to become like Christ and to be with Christ.

The sacrifice of Jesus Christ atoning for our sincerely repented sins is a awesome gift of God. It is the gift of God the Father, and it is the gift of the Son.

Reconciliation with God himself is a gift of God. Forgiveness is a gift of God. The Holy Spirit is a gift of God. And the fruit of the Holy Spirit is faith in God and eternal salvation; IF we continue in our commitment to God to STOP sinning, and continue to follow that Spirit into fully internalizing the very nature of God!

"We are His workmanship, created in Christ Jesus unto **good works**." That is, Jesus Christ created us to **do good works; which are the keeping of EVERY Word of God.**

Good works as defined by God is to live by every Word of God the Father and Jesus Christ! For, as Jesus said, "only God is good."

True good works are NOT doing what we think is right or good!

True good works are to live by the Word and Will of God Almighty as defined by the Word of God.

2:11 Wherefore, remember, that ye, being in time past, gentiles in the flesh, who are called uncircumcision by that which is called the circumcision in the flesh made by hands. **2:12** That at that time ye were without Christ, being aliens from the commonwealth of Israel, and strangers from the covenants of promise, having no hope, and without God in the world:

Both those of physical Israel and the physical Gentiles, who are called out and faithful to follow the whole Word of God, have become a new spiritual nation of priests and kings, full of the marvelous LIGHT of the Word of God, forever!

> **1 Peter 2:9** But **ye are a chosen generation, a royal priesthood, an holy nation, a peculiar** [special] **people;** that ye should shew forth the praises of him who hath called you out of darkness into his marvellous light;
>
> **Galatians 2:13** But, now, in Christ Jesus, he who sometimes were afar off, [those who were far off from God] are brought near [reconciled to God the Father] by the blood of Christ **2:14** for he is our peace who hath made both one and hath broken down the middle wall of partition between us.

We who were wicked in sin have been reconciled to God by the calling of God to sincere repentance and the removal of the veil of sin which has separated us from God through the sacrifice of Christ.

The veil in the temple which partitioned off the holy place the inner sanctuary of God from the people represented the veil of sin that separates us from God the Father.

Jesus Christ through his sacrifice; tore that veil apart, revealing that sincerely repented PAST sins could be removed by the application of his sacrifice, thus opening the way for the sincerely repentant to be reconciled to God the Father.

The symbolism of the tearing of the veil in the temple at the death of Christ is that the sacrifice of Jesus Christ could atone for and remove the sincerely repented sin which separates us from God, thereby reconciling us to God and allowing us access directly to God the Father.

Jesus Christ made peace between us and God the Father, by breaking down the partition of sin that separates us from the Father in heaven!

Ephesians 2:13 But now in Christ Jesus ye who sometimes were far off are made nigh by the blood of Christ. **2:14** For he is our peace, who hath made both [The sacrifice of the Lamb of God, reconciles the sincerely repentant with God the Father.] one, and hath broken down the middle wall of partition between us;

2:15 Having abolished in his flesh [by his sacrifice] the enmity, even the [the penalty of death which we owe for breaking the] law of commandments contained in ordinances; for to make in himself [to reconcile the sinful person to God by his sacrifice] of twain one new man [a new being in complete unity with God], so making peace; **2:16** And that he might reconcile both [reconcile the two, man and God] unto God in one body [in unity with God] by the cross [by his sacrifice], having slain the enmity [destroyed the division of sin between God and man] thereby: **2:17** And came and preached peace to you which were afar off [the Gentiles], and to them that were nigh [the Jews].

Having paid the penalty for our sins by giving up his life for sinners; Jesus Christ paid the penalty for those sins and reconciled repentant sinners to and brought them into complete unity with God the Father; thereby bringing two separate and opposite entities, the sinner and God, into complete unity!

2:18 For **through him we both have access by one Spirit unto the Father. 2:19** Now therefore ye are no more strangers and foreigners, but fellowcitizens with the saints, and of the household of God;

Through repentance and the application of the Passover sacrifice of Jesus Christ the Lamb of God, we have access to God the Father and the very Spirit and nature of God.

2:20 And are built upon the foundation of the apostles and prophets, Jesus Christ himself being the chief corner stone; **2:21** In whom all the building fitly framed together groweth unto an holy temple in the Lord: **2:22** In whom ye also are builded together for an habitation of God through the Spirit.

We must set aside all worldliness and build in ourselves a NEW PERSON, built on the solid foundation of the Word of God; WITHOUT compromise or any toleration of sin. We must not tolerate sin to be united with the sinful when our calling is to learn to abhor all sin for the sake of UNITY with GOD!

It is through sincere repentance and the application of Christ's sacrifice that we are reconciled to God the Father and can receive the gift of God's Spirit; and, thereby, have direct access to God the Father.

The collective body of those with God's Spirit is built upon the foundation of Jesus Christ and the whole Word of God: And the Apostles and Prophets were the ones who wrote the Word of God.

Moses was a prophet. The prophets wrote what some would call the Old Testament and the apostles wrote what some would call the New Testament.

The Bible is one cohesive whole and the New Testament merely explains and builds on the Old Testament.

The term apostles and prophets is a reference to all of the Holy Scriptures. The spiritual Ekklesia is built on the Holy Scriptures and not on the words of myself or any other man.

We should always be standing on ALL of the Holy Scriptures, "on the apostles and prophets and Jesus Christ. In whom, all the building fitly framed together grows in to a holy temple in the Lord. In whom, ye also are builded together for an habitation of God through the spirit."

The temple is the dwelling place of God; and, through God's Spirit dwelling in us, we become a spiritual temple of God. Then if we are faithfully submissive to God, and follow where God's Spirit leads and we passionately live by every Word of God, God's Spirit will dwell in us and we will have the sure hope of a resurrection to eternal life in spirit form.

Ephesians 3

Ephesians 3:1 For this cause I Paul, the prisoner of Jesus Christ for you Gentiles, **3:2** If ye have heard of the dispensation of the grace of God which is given me to you-ward: **3:3** How that by revelation he made known unto me the mystery; (as I wrote afore in few words, **3:4 Whereby, when ye read, ye may understand my knowledge in the mystery of Christ) 3:5 Which in other ages was not made known unto the sons of men,** as it is now revealed unto his holy apostles and prophets by the Spirit; effectual working of his power.

Far more than being only about circumcision or racism, Paul is explaining the mystery of the doctrine of salvation through Jesus Christ in this Epistle.

3:6 That the gentiles should be fellow heirs and of the same body, [that is, that the Gentiles should enter the same body (the Ekklesia) of Christ], that they should all be made one in Christ [The faithful are to be in complete unity with God the Father and Jesus Christ, and therefore in unity with each other.] and partakers of his promise in Christ by the gospel

The true gospel is the gospel of salvation through sincere repentance, the application of the sacrifice of Christ the Lamb of God, a dedicated zeal to learn and to keep the whole Word of God and complete unity with Jesus

Christ and with God the Father; which brings the promise of a resurrection to spirit and eternal life.

3:7 whereof I [Paul] was made a minister according to the gift of the grace of God, given unto me by the official working of his power.

Paul was called by God in God's mercy, just as we were also called out of sin to come to God the Father through Christ, and to follow the Father in Christ-like zeal to live by every Word of God.

3:8 Unto me, whom am less than the least of all saints, is this grace given that I should preach among the gentiles the unsearchable riches [the doctrine of salvation] of Christ. **3:9** And, to make all men see what is the fellowship of the mystery which from the beginning of the world hath bee hid in God **who created all things by Jesus Christ.**

Paul said that God created all things by the one who became Jesus Christ. Jesus Christ created all things and was the very Implementing Creator fulfilling the plan of God the Father.

3:10 To the intent that now unto the principalities and powers in heavenly places might be known by the church [the called out Ekklesia might know God] the manifold wisdom of God, **3:11** According to the eternal purpose which he purposed in Christ Jesus our Lord: **3:12** In whom we have boldness and access with confidence by the faith of him.

Paul was called to make known the mystery of the purpose and the plan of God and the mystery of the true doctrine of salvation.

The faithfully obedient to our heavenly Father have access to God the Father with boldness and confidence; knowing that we are not accessing the Father to encounter wrath and fury over our past disobedience.

Knowing that our past disobedience has been sincerely repented of and atoned for and has been forgiven and that God the Father loves us so much that he gave his Son for us; we can approach God our heavenly Father boldly and have access to him with confidence.

3:13 Wherefore, I desire that ye faint not at my tribulations and my troubles, for you, which is your glory.

Paul said, do not be upset or offended over my sufferings which are for your good [I suffer to preach to you the gospel of salvation so that you might be glorified],

3:14 for this cause I bow my knees unto the Father of our Lord Jesus Christ **3:15** of whom **the whole family** [that is, the family of God the

Father] in heaven and earth is named, **3:16** That **he would grant you according to the riches of his glory to be strengthened with might by his spirit** in the inner man.

Paul prayed as we all should pray, that God would deliver the people out of sin and into godliness and grant them his Spirit and eternal salvation.

3:17 That Christ [through the Holy Spirit] may dwell in your hearts by faith [Belief in the whole Word of God, combined with the works of faith to live by every Word of God.], that ye be rooted and grounded in love [which is obedience to God],

> **1 John 5:3** For **this is the love of God, that we keep his commandments**: and his commandments are not grievous.

Ephesians 3:18 may be able to comprehend, to understand, with all saints what is the breadth, the length, and depth and height. **3:19** And to know the love of Christ which passes knowledge that ye might be filled with all the fullness of God [so that we can all become just like God the Father]

3:20 Now, unto him that is able to do exceedingly, abundantly above all that we ask or think, according to the power [the power of God's Holy Spirit which is in those who are dedicated and passionately obedient to the whole Word of God] that works in us, **3:21** unto him be glory in the church by Christ Jesus, throughout all ages, world without end. Amen.

Paul is hoping and praying. and encouraging the called out; so that they will understand and fully comprehend the tremendous love that God the Father and Jesus Christ had and have, for Christ to give himself for all people and not just his own brethren in Judah for he was born of the flesh of Judah, but for all mankind, for the Gentiles and all humanity.

Paul wants us to begin to comprehend and to understand the breadth, the length, the depth, and the height of the love of Christ who gave himself for all peoples; and to understand the love of God the Father who gave his only son, his only begotten son, for all humanity while we were in rebellion against him.

Giving the life of the Lamb in the hope that when we understand the tremendous love that Jesus Christ and God the Father have for us, we will reciprocate that love and follow the Mighty Ones of our Salvation to dedicatedly love them and passionately desire to be like them; hungering and thirsting to internalize their nature, by keeping their Words of Life eternal.

Ephesians 4

Ephesians 4:1 I, therefore, the prisoner of the Lord beseech you that you should walk worthy of the vocation [live a godly life] where with [to which] you are called **4:2** With all lowliness [humility] and meekness, with longsuffering, forbearing one another in love; **4:2** Endeavoring to keep the unity of the spirit and the bond of peace.

Our unity is to be with God and that unity comes from living by every Word of God through the power of God's Spirit. We are to be united with God through the indwelling of the Holy Spirit which inspires the enthusiastic keeping of the whole Word of God.

Godly unity is not some emotional attachment to friends and some organization, or tolerating the sin that separates us from God for the sake of unity with people! Our unity is to be with God Almighty; which then brings unity with other like minded persons!

4:4 There is one body [one spiritual organism consisting of those faithful to God wherever they are] and one spirit even as you are called in one hope of your calling.

There is one spiritual Ekklesia, or one body of Christ but many parts.

3:5 One Lord, one faith, one baptism, **4:6** one God and Father of all who is above all and though all and in you all. **4:7** But anyone of us is given grace according to the measure of the gift of Christ. **4:8** Wherewith, he sayeth, when he ascends upon high he led captivity captive and gave gifts [salvation] unto men.

The true Ekklesia of God is not any corporate organization! It consists of all those who have responded to the Father's call; accepted the atonement of Christ; committed to obey God the Father and Jesus Christ forever; and are becoming ONE in complete unity with God the Father and Jesus Christ, through a diligent passionate living by Every Word of God; WITHOUT COMPROMISE and WITHOUT TOLERATING ANY DEFILEMENT OF SIN!

4:9 (Now, that he ascended what is it; but that he **also descended first** into the lower parts of the earth [the grave]?

That is, the Being that created all things, first descended from heaven unto the earth and then descended into the grave, before ascending back to God.

The Creator descended first unto the earth after giving up his God-hood and being made flesh, and then he was killed descending into the parts of the earth I.E. the grave; and then he was resurrected and ascended back up to God the Father.

4:10 He that descended is the same, also, that ascended up far above all heavens, that he might fill all things.)

The Being who created humanity, gave up his God-hood to be made flesh as Jesus Christ and descended to the earth to dwell among men; to learn through living a physical life what life as men in the flesh is like, to learn about the trials and tribulations and sufferings and joys of men. And after atoning for the sins of men, Christ ascended up to rejoin his Father!

He that descended is the same also that ascended again up far above all heavens and fulfilled all things written of him.

A list of offices

This is it is a list of various offices of responsibilities or administrative functions.

4:11 And, he gave some apostles and some prophets and some evangelists and some pastors and teachers **4:12** for the perfecting of the saints for the work of ministry, for the edifying of the body of Christ. **4:13 Till we all come in the unity of the faith and of the knowledge of the Son of God**

unto a perfect man and to the measure of the stature of the fullness of Christ.

God has given us teachers and helpers and guides to help us to become perfect — to help us to become like God the Father and Jesus Christ.

They are older brothers whose job is to focus us on God the Father and Jesus Christ and to teach us God's ways to help us to internalize every Word of God [which Word defines what God is]; so that we can internalize the very nature of God and become just like God in our attitude, words and actions!

The minute anyone says "tolerate sin," or "a little compromise doesn't matter Christ understands and will overlook it": SUCH MEN HAVE CEASED TO BE MEN OF GOD; and HAVE BECOME FALSE PROPHETS AND FALSE TEACHERS; seeking to steal your crowns and lead you into the path of destruction!

It is our calling to become FULLY like God the Father and Jesus Christ: "**a perfect man reaching to achieve the full measure of the stature of the fullness of Christ**".

We are not to seek excuses for failing to become like Christ, who lived by every Word of God the Father; we are to diligently WORK to achieve our goal and seek that Jesus Christ would dwell within us and lead and strengthen us to overcome as HE overcame.

What did Christ do? He KEPT HIS FATHER'S WORD! Without a shadow of compromise! To be like him we must do what he did!

> **John 15:10 If ye keep my commandments, ye shall abide in my love; even as I have kept my Father's commandments, and abide in his love.**

Christ said, I have kept the Father's commandments; I have kept my Father's law: And, we are to become like Christ. **We are to "fulfill the measure of the stature of the fullness of Christ."**

We are to keep God's commandments fully, just as Jesus Christ did. He didn't keep those commandments so we wouldn't have to; He kept those commandments as our example: So, that we can learn from that example and fill up the measure of the stature of the fullness of Christ.

We are to follow Christ's example and to become like him, and become good children of God the Father just as Jesus Christ was [and is]: And being good obedient children we would be acceptable to God the Father.

The various offices and gifts given to members of the body are merely responsibilities to be helps to assist the brethren to become LIKE God the Father and Jesus Christ for our salvation and glorification in the resurrection.

People in such positions are to be respected as our helps, but they are not to be exalted as some kind of grand idol or little god! And they are to be followed ONLY as they follow God the Father and Jesus Christ.

Apostles, prophets, evangelists, pastors and teachers are offices of responsibility and not some carnal hierarchical system of authority. Yes the offices have some authority as long as the holders are acting and teaching according to the whole Word of God and are not departing from God's Word; **but the authority resides in God and the Word of God and not in the person. If any leader departs from God's Word, then his authority has departed from him!**

True apostles, prophets, evangelists, pastors and teachers will stand firmly upon the whole Word of God. False leaders will claim to be godly as they deceive you away from any zeal for the whole Word of God to follow themselves.

We are not to be foolish and follow the cunning craftiness of false teachers into every false way like ignorant spiritual children, we are to be filled with and stand unshakably on the whole Word of God.

Ephesians 4:14 That we henceforth be no more children, tossed to and fro, and carried about with every wind of doctrine, by the sleight of men, and cunning craftiness, whereby they lie in wait to deceive;

The true people of God speak the TRUTH of the Word of God, and they stand on God's Word to internalize the very nature of God the Father and grow to become holy as God is holy; to become like Jesus Christ our espoused spiritual Husband and God our Father in heaven.

4:15 But **speaking the truth in love, may grow up into him** [We are to grow to become like Jesus Christ and God the Father.] **in all things, which is the head, even Christ:**

The way to avoid being tricked and deceived by cunning men and by the tares sowed amongst the wheat, is to stand on the solid foundation of the whole Word of God and the Chief Cornerstone, Jesus Christ.

We must test the words of all men against the words of the scriptural apostles, and prophets and Jesus Christ: And by the apostles and prophets I am referring to the writers of the Holy Scriptures, I am not referring to some fellow who comes along saying; " I am an Apostle" and only saying that to get your attention and excite your admiration so that he can deceive you with cunning craftiness to follow himself. Remember that God calls things what they are: men seldom do.

Now, there may be some people who are truly sent by God as messengers and as apostles. **But, if they are, they will be utterly consistent with the Word of God** and they will have no fear and no concern about you testing what they say against the Word of God.

The only reason for a fellow not to like you testing what he says, is because he is not consistent with the Word of God. Such false men who say "Questioning me is questioning God" are liars: for we are commanded not to blindly follow men, and are told to question all men by the whole Word of God.

> **1 Thessalonians 5:21 Prove all things; hold fast that which is good.**

If we hold men up to the standard of God's Word: We are NOT questioning God at all!

A true man of God will say "go ahead and check up on me: Absolutely, I will be consistent with the Word of God and if I am not, then there is a problem and you better believe the Word of God, first."

Ephesians 4:16 From whom the whole body fitly joined together and compacted by that which every joint supplies according to the effectual working in the measure of every part [Every true part of the body works under the direction of the Head which is God the Father and Jesus Christ 1 Corinthians 11:3.], maketh increase of the body unto the edifying of itself in love.

The spiritual Ekklesia [the brotherhood] is the body of Christ. Every individual in that body should be cooperating and obeying the instructions of its HEAD Jesus Christ, and above Christ, God the Father; for the good of the body of the brotherhood and to edify [build up] the body of the called out to become godly and Christ-like!

Right now the Ekklesia is NOT listening to their HEAD, they are flopping about like a headless body; not standing on the sound doctrine of the Word of God and Jesus Christ, but instead standing on the false traditions of men and doing what each group thinks is right rather than doing what GOD SAYS IS RIGHT!

Zealous for men and organizations and cold for God to keep his Word! Hot in grand claims and lip-service and cold in the works of faith, which is diligent obedience to every Word of God; thus being a mixture of lukewarmness disgusting to Jesus Christ and to God the Father.

We are all about grand claims, lip service and appearances; being hot to follow idols of men, while being cold towards sound doctrine and any zeal to learn and to keep the whole Word of God.

We of the true called out, are not to walk [live and act] as spiritual Gentiles [the unconverted] who are blind to spiritual things]. We are to be diligent to follow the espoused Husband of our baptismal commitment to live by every Word of God the Father!

4:17 This I say, therefore, and testify in the Lord **that you, henceforth walk not as other gentiles walk or live, as other gentiles live, in the vanity of their mind, 4:18 having the understanding darkened being alienated from the life of God to the ignorance that is in them because of the blindness of their hearts.**

4:19 Who being past feeling, have given themselves unto lasciviousness, to work all uncleanness, with greediness 4:20 But ye have not so learned Christ; **4:21** If so be that ye have heard him, and have been taught by him, as the truth is in Jesus:

We are to put away all sin and we are NOT to tolerate or justify any willful sin in ourselves or in our assemblies!

We are to put off the sins of the past and we are to become new people in Christ; full of zeal to please and do the will and keep the Word of God the Father and Jesus Christ the espoused Husband of our baptismal commitment!

4:22 That ye put off concerning the former conversation [sinful conduct] the old man, which is corrupt according to the deceitful lusts; **4:23 And be renewed in the spirit of your mind; 4:24 And that ye put on the new man, which after God is created in righteousness and true holiness.**

Put away the life of sin and build a new person free from sin: A new person in Godliness; learning to follow the example of Jesus Christ and to become like Christ in true zeal for God the Father and all godliness.

4:25 Therefore, putting away lying, speak every man the truth with his neighbor for we are members one of another.

The biggest lie that is told, are that we should follow men who cast away parts of the scriptures to deceive the brethren into accepting men as idols coming between the brethren and Almighty God!

4:26 Be ye angry, and sin not: let not the sun go down upon your wrath: **4:27** Neither give place to the devil.

This simply means that, yes we can get upset over things that are wrong or evil, we can get angry at SIN, but we are not to lose control of ourselves. We are not to lose our balance and our sound mind. We are not to lose sound judgment and we are not to be angry without a righteous cause.

Let not the sun go down upon your wrath. Whenever there is a problem, we should never let it fester and grow in our minds! We should try to resolve it as soon as possible, before it grows out of all proportion in our minds.

We need to be man enough to take the bull by the horns, to be the leader, to be proactive instead of reactive; to be willing to take the first step in trying to resolve problems and difficulties and to follow the instructions of Jesus Christ in Matthew 18.

Neither give place to the devil. That is, don't lose your temper, do not lose your self- control and let the devil find a crack to get in your head and stir things up.

Maintain your self-control. It should be a given, that when one is angry, one should work off the adrenaline with exercise and then go to one's private place and take the problem to God, and then work to get and understand the true facts.

Only after that, the next step should be to go out and try and resolve the problem with the other person.

Get rid of that anger. Get rid of that temper. Work off the adrenaline. Go to God with it. Lay it out for Him and He will help you to get control of yourself and that will be a giant step forward in preparing you to reach out to the other party in resolving any problems as per Matthew 18.

24:8 Let him that stole steal no more: but rather let him labour, working with his hands the thing which is good, that he may have to give to him that needeth.

Corrupt communication means spreading falsehoods and false teachings, which lead people away from any zeal to keep the whole Word of God.

4:29 Let no corrupt communication proceed out of your mouth, but that which is good to the use of edifying [Speak things that are uplifting towards godliness and building up others towards holiness.], that it may minister grace unto the hearers.

We grieve the Holy Spirit by rejecting the truth of God's Word and rejecting any zeal for keeping the whole Word of God, preferring to follow idols of men and false traditions.

4:30 And grieve not **the Holy Spirit of God, whereby ye are sealed** unto the day of redemption.

The word sealed, means; marked or set apart and, we are set apart to godly holiness, if we have sincerely repented and are resolved to sin no more: Then God's Spirit will dwell within us.

We are supposed to be different from those people who do not have God's Spirit dwelling within them. Therefore, the Spirit of God within us is a seal and a mark by which we may be recognized as belonging to God, as being a godly person! And how is that seal visible to others? It is made visible by the things that we say and do! It is made manifest by the LIGHT of OUR EXAMPLE!

The example of most of today's spiritual Ekklesia is not one of godliness, but one of shameful carnality; of exalting our own false traditions above God's Word and exalting men and organizations above the Word of Almighty God.

Brethren, put away the animosity and jealousy from among you; learn to forgive others just as Jesus Christ and God the Father have forgiven us.

4:31 Let all bitterness, and wrath, and anger, and clamour, and evil speaking, be put away from you, with all malice: **4:32** And be ye kind one to another, tenderhearted, **forgiving one another, even as God for Christ's sake hath forgiven you.**

Ephesians 5

Ephesians 5:1 Be ye, therefore, followers of God as dear children. 5:2 And walk in love, as Christ also hath loved us, and hath given himself for us an offering and a sacrifice to God for a sweetsmelling savour.

We are to follow God like young children follow their parents. God is our Father. Follow him like an obedient and loving child. Walk [LIVE] in love as defined by the Word of God the Father. Keep the whole Word of God just as Jesus Christ kept God the Father's Word and has loved the Father and has loved us and has given himself for us, as a pleasant and acceptable sacrifice to God.

Christ gave himself wholly and wholeheartedly to God the Father and we should follow that example and also wholeheartedly live as Christ lived and lives.

5:3 But fornication [Pornea: including all disloyalty and idolatry] and uncleanness or covetousness, let it not be once named among you as becoming saints.

We are to flee from adultery and idolatry both physical and spiritual. Spiritual adultery and idolatry is to compromise with the Word of God and to follow idols of men and corporate entities above living by every Word of God.

5:4 Neither filthiness nor foolish talking nor jesting which are not convenient [appropriate] but rather giving of thanks.

This doesn't mean you can't have a good laugh. It does mean that you should avoid filthiness [uncleanness of deeds and words] and cruel, evil, or despicable kinds of language; racial jokes and slurs and sexual slurs and jokes; and even worse is the teaching of false doctrines and a lack of zeal to live by every Word of God.

The teaching that the Sabbath and High Days are holy, but that we can pollute them and walk all over them is Filthy Communication.

The teaching that people should obey the corporate church or any person in place of the scriptures is Filthy Communication. We should be clean minded and clean-spirited; wholeheartedly dedicated to "following the Lamb of God whithersoever he goeth."

5:5 For this you know that no whoremonger [including a spiritual whoremonger who runs after every false way] nor unclean person [spiritually a person polluted by any sin] nor covetous man who is an idolater, [Any person who allows anything to come between them and God; including the putting of men between themselves and God is an idolater and a spiritual adulterer.] has any inheritance in the kingdom of Christ and of God.

Be diligent to study and live by every Word of God no matter what anyone else says, in this way those who use clever words to deceive can be discerned by their departure from God's Word.

Have nothing to do with false teachers who do not teach a dedicated zeal to live by every Word of God. Be careful to judge by what they do and not by what they say, because many talk a good talk with which they cloak their false traditions.

5:6 Let no man deceive you with vain words for because of these things comes the wrath of God upon the children of disobedience. 5:7 Be not, therefore, partakers with them.

In times past, we were in the darkness of ignorance of the Word of God, but now God has called us into the light of his Word. Therefore let us remain in the light of God's Word and not allow ourselves to be deceived back into the darkness of living contrary to any part of the whole Word of God.

5:8 For ye were sometimes darkness but now are ye light in the Lord, walk as the children of light.

5:9 For the fruit of the spirit is in all goodness and righteousness and truth. **5:10** Proving what is acceptable unto God.

The Holy Spirit is truth and God is truth and God's Spirit leads us into those things that are acceptable to the LORD [YHVH], acceptable to God the Father and Jesus Christ, and God defines those things that are acceptable to him by his Word.

5:11 Have no fellowship with the unfruitful works of darkness but, rather, reprove them.

We are to reprove wickedness especially within the assembly and cast out the habitual sinner having nothing to do with them, because the works of darkness lead to decay and death.

Today we have become comfortable in our ruts and we do not realize that much that we do is evil according to the Word of God, and we do many things which are a disgrace and an offense to Almighty God.

The light reveals all things, and the light of the Word makes known all things.

Whosoever makes known the truth and rebukes all evil; is of God.

5:12 For it is a shame to even speak of those things which are done of them in secret. But all things that are reproved are made known by the light. **5:13** For whatsoever does make known or make manifest is light.

5:14 Wherefore he saith, Awake thou that sleepest, and arise from the dead, and Christ shall give thee light.

There are very many who hate those who expose and reprove the evils of today's religions. Like silly foolish children they close their eyes to the truth, but God will NOT close his eyes to the truth.

Brethren, ignorance is NOT bliss; for God has commanded his people to cast light on wickedness and reprove evil, so that people may have an opportunity to correct themselves before God corrects them!

If the Watchman does not reprove sin; he is a worthless watchman; for he has not warned us that our sin will result in our correction (Ezek 33)!

The Light of God reveals those things that are hidden and dissipates the darkness that obscures and hides sin!

To become like God, we MUST root out and destroy all sin, cleaning our spiritual temple completely, so that no defilement remains.

To hide our eyes from our sins is the broad road that will lead to our correction and ultimately to our destruction; if we do not repent of that wickedness!

5:15 See then that you walk circumspectly, not as fools, but as wise, **5:16** redeeming the time because the days are evil.

We should concentrate on the things of God while we can. Our physical lives are short and even though we might think that we are going to live forever, we will grow old very quickly without noticing.

We need to make the most of every hour of our lives, learning and living by the things of God and not wasting our lives in foolishness and the ways of wickedness. We NEED to spend our days seeking the truth of God and removing the evil within ourselves!

5:17 Wherefore, be ye not unwise or foolish but understanding what the will of the Lord is. **5:18** be not drunk with wine, wherein excess, but be filled with the spirit.

We are not to be drunkards and that can be extended to include becoming intoxicated with any other drug or narcotic. We are not to allow ourselves to become intoxicated and to lose control of our mental and physical abilities and faculties: And, we are not to waste our time in drunkenness and wantonness and such foolishness.

The greatest intoxicant is the spiritual intoxicant of PRIDE which intoxicates the mind [spirit] and lifts us up in our own sight. Spiritually we are not to intoxicate ourselves with our own false traditions and pride in our own supposed righteousness.

We are not to become intoxicated with the pleasures and false ways of this world; we are not to tempt ourselves with worldly pleasures or to make any physical thing our priority over perfecting ourselves and coming into total unity with God the Father and Jesus Christ. We are not to delight in false teachings and the imaginations of men.

We should be filled with the Spirit of God, which comes through obedience to the whole Word of God (Acts 5:32).

5:19 Speaking to yourselves in psalms and hymns and spiritual songs, singing and making melody in your heart to the Lord; **5:20** Giving thanks always for all things unto God and the Father in the name of our Lord Jesus Christ; **5:21** Submitting yourselves one to another in the fear of God.

Singing and making melody in our hearts to the Lord: If we are filled with God's Spirit and we are truly happy, we will rejoice, and that rejoicing will manifest itself in a happy bubbling over, singing; kind of attitude.

God's people should not be morose and dour and sour and long faced all the time. They should be happy people; happy that they are free from bondage to sin and the suffering and the eternal death that sin brings.

Not a shallow superficial happiness, but a deep seated joy in true security, trust and faith in the power of God our Father to keep his promises and deliver his loyal children from the grave to eternal life.

Oh, yes. Satan will bring persecution. But, we know that we will ultimately have deliverance by the power of God; whose power is unmatched by anyone or anything or all other things put together. Our Father in heaven is a strong fortress. And he has all power and he can and will deliver us, if we put him first. Therefore, we can rejoice in heart and in spirit, as we steadfastly face all our trials with absolute assurance and faith in the promises of God.

We should have more of a rejoicing and joyful attitude, rather than a sour kind of oh-woe-is-me attitude. We should be happy in the things of God and, we should be giving thanks, always, for all things; unto God and the Father, in the name of our Lord Jesus Christ.

One of the great sins is ingratitude. We should be thankful to God for the things that he has given us and the blessings he has provided or promised.

One of the greatest blessings being our very life existence and the potential for eternal life as a spirit, forgiven from sin with a strong fully healthy body and mind!

"Submit one to another in the fear of God." That is, cooperate with one another, forgive one another, give place to the other if they have a better idea that you, be cooperative and supportive of each other, as long as doing so is fully consistent with living by every Word of God.

NEVER give place to another for one fraction of a second if we must compromise with our relationship with our beloved Father to do so!

5:22 Wives submit yourselves unto your husbands as you would submit unto God. **5:23** For the husband is the head of the wife even as Christ is the head of the church. And, he is the savior of the body.

Jesus Christ the Lamb of God, is the Savior of the godly faithful.

The sincerely repentant brethren, those that respond to the Father's calling with sincere repentance, who come under Christ's sacrifice and have been given the Holy Spirit of God and who commit themselves to stop sinning; those people will be saved by Christ who is their Savior.

Does that mean we don't have problems? Of course not — but it means that we will keep on trying and overcoming (Pro 24:16), and ultimately we will be changed and we will never see or taste of death again once we are changed to spirit.

The spiritual Ekklesia is to be subject to God the Father and Jesus Christ; and if a corporate church is not subject to Christ [keeping the teachings and commandments of Christ and living by every Word of God; they are NOT a part of Christ's body!].

5:24 Therefore as the church [the spiritual Ekklesia, the various converted brethren] is subject unto Christ, so let the wives be to their own husbands in every thing.

Wives and children are to be subject to their husbands [or fathers] "In the Lord, " always putting God first and after that their fathers and husbands.

5:25 Husbands, love your wives, even as Christ also loved the church, and gave himself for it;

Christ gave his very life for the good of his collective bride and we husbands are not to bully our wives but we are to give ourselves for the good of our wives. Husbands are NOT to bully their wives; they are not to be selfish, they are to be dedicated to the good of their wives and families.

5:26 That he might sanctify and cleanse it with the washing of water by the word, **5:27** That he might present it to himself a glorious church, not having spot, or wrinkle, or any such thing; but that it should be holy and without blemish.

The true spiritual Ekklesia consists of those who are called by God the Father, who have sincerely repented and resolved not to sin anymore, who have been atoned for by the sacrifice of Christ, and who have been given God's Spirit.

The true spiritual Ekklesia is not a corporate organization, it is not one group or another group. It is the individuals, and collectively all the individuals [regardless of corporate church affiliation] who are filled with the Spirit of God and passionately live by every Word of God.

Husbands love your wives and live for their good, just as Jesus Christ also loves the bride [the spiritual Ekklesia] and lived for and gave himself for us.

We look so much at the sacrifice of Christ and at his death and resurrection, and, this should be so; because that is a tremendous gift from Christ and from God the Father: But, there is another point which is that Christ LIVED for the spiritual Ekklesia, his bride. He lived to bring sinners to repentance. He lived to teach the way to true holiness, to true Godliness, to justice, peace, truth, harmony and balance in all things.

Jesus Christ lived a life of teaching and service, of setting an example for the people; and we need to focus not just on the death and resurrection of Christ but on his life of total faithful uncompromising obedience and service to God the Father for the good of the bride. It was his sinless passionate obedience to every Word of God that made Christ the Lamb of God and an effectual sacrifice for the sins of the world!

Husbands we must live for God and for the families that God has given us in the same way that Christ lived for his Father; and lived and died for his called out bride the spiritual Ekklesia. We must follow the example that Christ set; and be willing to take it all the way and die, if necessary, for God the Father and for the good of our families as well.

We are to give ourselves totally for God the Father and for the good of our family; just as Jesus Christ gave himself totally, for his Father and for the good of his bride, his family.

That he might sanctify and cleanse it with the washing of water by the Word, so that he might present his people, his bride; to himself [and to his Father] — a glorious bride, not having a spot or wrinkle or any such thing; not having any blemish [of uncleanness or sin] at all.

We should be pure from all defilement [blemishes] of sin and all evil.

Paul speaks here about a man and a woman joining together to become one flesh. Paul refers to that as an analogy that Christ is to become one with his bride — one in complete unity with his faithful, in heart, mind, spirit, attitude and actions.

The saints are, in fact, the collective spiritual bride of Christ. They are to present themselves as chaste, pure virgins free from pollution by any false ways or uncleanness of sin to Christ at their resurrection to spirit.

To be "chaste, pure virgins" means that we are not to be polluted by following after other lovers, and not following any other or allowing anything to come between ourselves and our espoused Husband.

DO NOT learn the false ungodly traditions of men, to believe them or to do them; that is spiritual fornication and idolatry!

Jesus Christ becomes one in complete unity with the faithful and we become one in complete unity with him and God the Father through internalizing and living by every Word of God!

When we are judged and chosen by God for our absolute loyalty to, and unity of mind and spirit with God our Father and our espoused Husband Jesus Christ; we will be changed to spirit and will become spirit as Christ is spirit; then our unity of marriage becomes complete (Rev 15, 19).

This is very much what the relationship between a man and his wife is intended to portray. The physical relationship of marriage is intended to be a teaching analogy to demonstrate to us the kind of relationship that we should have with Jesus Christ and with God the Father.

Wives should be obedient, faithful, cooperative, passionately loving of their husbands; the kind of wife that Christ would accept as his own bride! Likewise we should all be obedient, faithful, cooperative, passionate and loving of our espoused Husband Jesus Christ!

The example of Jesus Christ shows us the kind of fathers and husbands we should be! Husbands are to nourish and cherish their wives as Christ nourishes and cherishes his bride.

5:28 So ought men to love their wives as their own bodies. He that loveth his wife loveth himself. **5:29** For no man ever yet hated his own flesh; but **nourisheth and cherisheth it, even as the Lord the church: 5:30** For we are members of his body, of his flesh, and of his bones. **5:31** For this cause shall a man leave his father and mother, and shall be joined unto his wife, and they two shall be one flesh.

Marriage is not a domination game, nor is it an "I have my rights game;" marriage is about cooperating and working together for the good of the whole family. Marriage is a classroom to learn about the relationship that Christ wants with his people. Marriage is also a classroom to learn leadership, patience, and ultimately the meaning of true godly love, and much else

5:32 This is a great mystery, but I speak concerning Christ and the church. Nevertheless, let everyone of you in particular so love his wife, even, as he loves himself. And, the wife see that she reverence her husband.

Wives should esteem their husbands and husbands should esteem their wives, even as we in the faith should be esteeming our espoused Husband, Jesus Christ, who loved us and gave his life for us.

Ephesians 6

Ephesians 6:1 Children obey your parents in the Lord (Ex 20:12, Deu 5:16) for this is right. **6:2** Honour they father and mother which is the first commandment with promise. **6:3** That it may be well with thee and thou must live long on the earth.

We have the promise that if we obey our physical parents and our heavenly Father then it will ultimately be well with us and we shall live for eternity. We are to obey our heavenly Father first and our physical parents after that, just as wives are to obey their heavenly Father first and after that their own husbands.

This same command requires us to obey our heavenly Father first, and after that to obey teachers of men ONLY as they are consistent with the whole Word of God our Father in heaven.

If we call the Sabbath holy and then pollute it because some man said it was alright; know that we are breaking the commandment to honor our Father as well! To follow any person in breaking the Word of God our Father in heaven is the sin of idolatry and breaks the commandment to honor our Father!

6:4 Ye fathers provoke not your children to wrath but bring them up in the nurture and admonition of the Lord.

Physical fathers are to teach their children godly holiness, to guide them, to lead them, to nudge them in the positive direction of true Godliness. Don't bully them or abuse them, but gently and firmly teach them in godly love

Yes, sometimes discipline is necessary, but for the most part it is patient loving guidance and instruction that is needed; and that kind of attitude and patient guidance and love is to begin from the very birth of the child.

Even as a very young child, we should be spending time with that child, guiding, teaching, loving, and patiently pointing them in positive directions. An early start will eliminate most of the need for discipline later on. We won't have to discipline all the time if we start very early to establish a positive and loving relationship and to establish positive attitudes and positive behavioral patterns in a child, as young as possible.

6:5 Servants be obedient to them, that are your masters [yet, still putting God first] according to the flesh, with fear and trembling, in singleness of your heart, as unto Christ;

This is not just about a master- slave relationship, but is about any kind of relationship which involves serving others.

6:6 Not with eye service as men pleasers; but as the servants of Christ, doing the will of God from the heart;

Don't just be nice when they are around, don't just be working when they are watching; but be faithful whether they are watching or not.

6:7 Not, with eye-services as menpleasers but as the servants of Christ, doing the will of God from the heart. **6:8** Knowing that whatsoever good thing any man doeth, the same shall he receive of the Lord, whether he be bond or free.

Seek to do what is right and good, wholeheartedly with a good conscience, serving as if you were serving God and not men only, because we are serving others in obedience to God our Father.

We will receive our reward from God for whatever we do, whether it is God's correction for evil or God's blessing for doing good. We will be judged as to whether we are good or evil by God: And, we will receive our reward in either case, according to our conduct.

6:9 and ye masters, do the same thing unto your servants. Forbearing, threatening, knowing that your master also is in heaven neither is there respect of persons is with him.

No converted person is to bully and dominate others for his own advantage, including his wife and children, and a woman should not seek personal advantage over her husband and children. The duty of every person is to serve God and mankind for the advantage of our families and the brotherhood, so that they may attain to godly holiness and become a fit part of the collective bride of Christ.

6:10 Finally, my brethren, be strong in the Lord, and in the power of his might. **6:11** Put on the whole armour of God, that ye may be able to stand against the wiles of the devil.

Seek spiritual strength from God and God's Spirit, to give us victory in the good fight against Satan and sin.

Remember as you see the Ekklesia apostatizing, that apostates and persecutors have been misled by the devil into thinking that they are doing good; and if any attack you, your fight is not really with them, but with Satan the great deceiver.

6:12 For we wrestle not against flesh and blood, but against principalities, against powers, against the rulers of the darkness of this world, **against spiritual wickedness** in high places.

6:13 Wherefore take unto you the whole armour of God, that ye may be able to withstand in the evil day, and having done all, to stand.

Our persecutors are not really those people who are abusing us. They are the spiritual forces that are influencing such people and inspiring them to do such things that are the true source of all our trials.

When we are being persecuted we are to stand firm on the whole Word of God throughout all our trials. Then we will stand in the resurrection before the throne of God (Rev 15).

God's Word is truth (John 17:17) and we are to clothe ourselves with righteousness; which is the zealous keeping of the truth, the whole Word of God!

6:14 Stand therefore, having your loins girt about with truth, and having on the breastplate of righteousness;

Having our feet shod with the gospel of peace refers to being at peace with God and refers to our walk [life] in the gospel of salvation. The Gospel of Peace is salvation by sincere repentance, a baptismal commitment to sin no more and the application of the sacrifice of Jesus Christ justifying us; and then to live our lives by every Word of God and live at peace with God the Father always.

6:15 And your feet shod with the preparation of the gospel of peace; **6:16** Above all, taking the shield of faith, wherewith ye shall be able to quench all the fiery darts of the wicked.

The Gospel is the good news of the way to reconciliation and peace with GOD the FATHER!

The Gospel is about sincere repentance, a commitment to sin no more and the application of the atoning sacrifice of the Lamb of God, reconciling us with God the Father; and it is about unity with God by continuing in that relationship, through a diligent rejection of sin [which sin separates us from God] and a passionate uncompromising keeping of the whole Word and Will of God! This is the foundation of peace and unity between man and God and true unity among like-minded people!

If we are faithful to live by every Word of God, we will know and trust and believe in God and we will obey God our Father in heaven.

God will defend us and take care of us with his great power and if he allows us to suffer for a time it is so that we might learn something important, and he will raise us up on that day and change us to spirit and we shall never taste of death again.

6:17 And take the helmet of salvation, and **the sword of the Spirit, which is the word of God**: **6:18** Praying always with all prayer and supplication in the Spirit, [pray with a whole heart, with all our heart and spirit, with intensity] and watching thereunto with all perseverance and supplication for all saints;

Take the helmet of salvation and valiantly wield the sword of the Spirit, which is the truth of the whole Word of God. God's Spirit gives us understanding of the Word of God, the Holy Scriptures: And, the Holy Scriptures are the sword of truth with which we fight sin.

We are to fight sin and evil with the sword of truth and not with bloodshed.

Only that which is evil needs to fear the sharp two edged sword of the LIGHT of Truth! For the Light of Truth exposes the wicked things hidden in darkness; and the sharp two edged sword of God's Word destroys all that is evil from before him.

The workers of evil deeds try to hide in darkness and obscurity and they HATE being exposed by the light of truth!

The truly godly will welcome the Light of the Truth; for they are the children of the Light: While the wicked will hate the Light of the Truth for it exposes their sin.

6:19 And for me, that utterance may be given unto me, that I may open my mouth boldly, to make known the mystery of the gospel, **6:20** For which I am an ambassador in bonds: that therein I may speak boldly, as I ought to speak.

Tychicus is sent to take the letter to the Ephesians and to inform them more fully.

6:21 But that ye also may know my affairs, and how I do, Tychicus, a beloved brother and faithful minister in the Lord, shall make known to you all things: **6:22** Whom I have sent unto you for the same purpose, that ye might know our affairs, and that he might comfort your hearts.

The blessing of peace is first and foremost, that we be at peace with God our Father and not be separated from God by any sin; for we are promised trial and tribulation in this evil world and not peace (John 16:33).

6:23 Peace be to the brethren, and love with faith, from God the Father and the Lord Jesus Christ. **6:24** Grace [Mercy] be with all them that love our Lord Jesus Christ in sincerity. Amen

Philippians

Philippians 1

The Philippians lived in the city of Philippi, which is a city near Neapolis in Macedonia. Paul and Timothy are writing this Epistle together, just like Paul and Timothy wrote to the Colossians together.

Philippians 1:1 Paul and Timotheus, the servants of Jesus Christ, to all the saints in Christ Jesus which are at Philippi, with the bishops and deacons: **1:2** Grace be unto you, and peace, from God our Father, and from the Lord Jesus Christ.

1:3 I thank my God upon every remembrance of you, **1:4** Always in every prayer of mine for you all making request with joy, **1:5** For your fellowship in the gospel from the first day until now; **1:6** Being confident of this very thing, that he which hath begun a good work in you will perform it until the day of Jesus Christ:

Paul tells the Philippians that he is very confident in their sincere repentance and diligence to attain to the salvation of the gospel, and that he is sure that they will succeed and overcome and endure until the end.

1:7 Even as it is meet for me to think this of you all, because I have you in my heart; inasmuch as both in my bonds, and in the defence and confirmation of the gospel, ye all are partakers of my grace.

Paul calls the faithful and zealous for God "fellow partakers" of the same grace [the calling and salvation of God through Jesus Christ] as he himself, and assures them of how deeply he longs to be with them. Together they long to be with each other [Paul and the Philippians], for they are both full of the same Spirit of God the Father and Jesus Christ and they have the same deep mutual passionate love for God the Father and the whole Word of God.

1:8 For God is my record, how greatly I long after you all in the bowels of Jesus Christ. **1:9** And this I pray, that your love may abound yet more and more in knowledge and in all judgment;

Paul prays for them that their love for God and for keeping every Word of God [which defines godly love] will abound all the greater and bear fruit in an increase of knowledge, understanding and the sound judgment of God. I also pray that the same blessings will be poured out on the faithful and diligent for God.

1:10 That ye may approve [that you may accept, diligently seek and grow in the spiritual things which are acceptable to God] things that are excellent; that ye may be sincere and without offence [that you may be without sin or any offense against God, in the day of judgment] till the day of Christ.

Paul is hopeful that their [our] love of godliness may abound and that their [our] good works of faith should abound, and that they/we should excel and be sincere without any sin or offense against God and be well pleasing to God, always.

1:11 Being filled with the fruits of righteousness, which are by Jesus Christ, unto the glory and praise of God.

The whole Word of God is righteousness, defining God who is righteousness; and our duty is to internalize and be filled with the very nature of God, which is achieved through the passionate keeping of every Word of God.

1:12 But I would ye should understand, brethren, that the things which happened unto me have fallen out rather unto the furtherance of the gospel; **1:13** So that my bonds in Christ are manifest in all the palace, and in all other places;

Paul tells the Philippians not to be discouraged by his trials, telling them that because of the charges against him and his imprisonment, the Gospel has been spread abroad.

Everyone in the palace and people throughout the land were hearing of his situation and were hearing the Gospel, so that his imprisonment is actually working to further the spreading of the Gospel. Paul's imprisonment and courage are also inspiring others to take a stand for godliness.

1:14 And many of the brethren in the Lord, waxing confident by my bonds, are much more bold to speak the word without fear.

Some preach salvation through Christ for personal reasons, while others preach the truth in sincerity and true godly love. Paul set us an example that he does not care who preached the truth; as long as the truth is preached!

1:15 Some indeed preach Christ even of envy and strife; and some also of good will: **1:16** The one preach Christ of contention, not sincerely, supposing to add affliction to my bonds: **1:17** But the other of love, knowing that I am set for the defence of the gospel. **1:18** What then? notwithstanding, every way, whether in pretence, or in truth, **Christ is preached; and I therein do rejoice, yea, and will rejoice.**

Paul said that he lives and dies for God the Father and Jesus Christ, and declares that to remain diligent in so doing will be his salvation.

The same is true of us: Our salvation rests in our being diligent to live and die for God the Father just as Jesus Christ did. We should do likewise; presenting our wholehearted service as a fitting, pleasant and acceptable burnt offering to God the Father the Almighty!

Let us be bold for God to learn and to live by every Word of God and to be well studied and grounded in sound doctrine so that we are able to explain and teach the truth of God to all who ask us, just as Paul was and did.

1:19 For I know that this shall turn to my salvation through your prayer, and the supply of the Spirit of Jesus Christ, **1:20** According to my earnest expectation and my hope, that in nothing I shall be ashamed, but that with all boldness, as always, so now also Christ shall be magnified in my body, whether it be by life, or by death.

Paul longs with all his heart for his life's struggles to end, yet he knows that he is needed for the preaching of the Gospel of Salvation so that others may also converted to godliness.

1:21 For to me to live is Christ, and to die is gain [The godly will be resurrected to eternal life with Christ.]. **1:22** But if I live in the flesh, this is the fruit of my labour: yet what I shall choose I wot not. **1:23** For I am in a strait betwixt two, having a desire to depart, and to be with Christ; which is far better: **1:24** Nevertheless **to abide in the flesh is more needful for you**.

Paul lived to please God, just as Jesus Christ lived to please God the Father; and we should do likewise.

> **John 4:34** Jesus saith unto them, My meat is to do the will of him that sent me, and to finish his work.

Philippians 1:25 And having this confidence, I know that I shall abide and continue with you all for your furtherance and joy of faith; **1:26** That your rejoicing may be more abundant in Jesus Christ for me by my coming to you again.

Paul's joy in life was to serve and please God, and to teach the things of God and encourage people to a zeal for God and spiritual salvation. Paul encourages the Philippians and us today, to stand fast in wholehearted unity with God and the whole Word of God.

1:27 Only let your conversation be as it becometh the gospel of Christ: that whether I come and see you, or else be absent, I may hear of your affairs, that **ye stand fast in one spirit, with one mind striving together for the faith** [which includes the works of faith] **of the gospel**;

Fear [exalt] no man, but question every word of men by the Word of God. Exalt God and fear to displease Almighty God.

Many leaders and elders today think that they should be exalted and that the brethren should blindly follow whatever they say without question. Do not be afraid of them, for in setting themselves up above the Word of God they have made themselves the adversaries of God and the deceivers of the people of God.

1:28 And **in nothing terrified** [Do not be terrified by men in any thing, no matter what titles they claim.] **by your adversaries**: which is to them an evident token of perdition, [They think that we are damned if we do not fear men. Yet, to question the words of men by the Word of God and to cleave to God's Word alone, safeguards our salvation!] but to you of salvation, and that of God.

Such men are so full of themselves that they suppose that our lack of exalting and fearing men is a sign that we are damned, when it is exalting and fearing men above the Word of God which brings damnation.

Jesus warned that many false teachers would seek to deceive the Ekklesia. Matthew 24:4 is a warning to the disciples of Christ, not to the world which has always been deceived! The Gospels and Epistles are full of warnings to the brethren, to beware; for many deceivers shall enter the assemblies and lead many brethren astray!

> **Matthew 24:4** And Jesus answered and said unto them [his disciples], Take heed that no man deceive you **24:5** For many shall come in my name, saying, I am Christ; and shall deceive many [of the brethren].

Every one who believes Jesus Christ and has the works of faith, which is to live by every Word of God in Christ-like zeal, and who refuses to follow human deceivers; will be persecuted by the wicked.

Philippians 1:29 For unto you it is given in the behalf of Christ, not only to believe on him, but also to suffer for his sake; **1:30** Having the same conflict which ye saw in me, and now hear to be in me.

Philippians 2

Philippians 2:1 If there be therefore any consolation in Christ, if any comfort of love, if any fellowship of the Spirit, if any bowels and mercies, **2:2 Fulfil ye my joy, that ye be likeminded, having the same love, being of one accord, of one mind** [with Almighty God].

Paul admonishes the Philippians to be like-minded together in complete unity with God the Father and with Jesus Christ, so that they will all be like-minded with God and with each other.

He calls on all of the brotherhood to work together, each one esteeming the others above himself. Yes, that means that the elders and leaders should also have the same godly humility and be subject to God, esteeming the brethren.

2:3 Let nothing be done through strife or vainglory; but in lowliness of mind [humility] **let each esteem other better than themselves.**

Let each one be helpful to others and not be solely focused on himself alone.

2:4 Look not every man on his own things, but every man also on the things of others.

We are to be of one mind with Jesus Christ who is of one mind in complete unity with God the Father.

2:5 Let this mind be in you, which was also in Christ Jesus: 2:6 Who, being in the form of God, thought it not robbery to be equal with God:

Jesus Christ was a part of the God family and gave up his God-hood to be made flesh and was obedient to God the Father to his very death while in the flesh.

2:7 But made himself of no reputation, and took upon him the form of a servant, and was made in the likeness of men: 2:8 And being found in fashion as a man, he humbled himself, and became obedient unto death, even the death of the cross.

Because of his life of obedience and his death in obedience to God the Father, Jesus Christ was resurrected to spirit and exalted over all powers that exist [except God the Father himself].

2:9 Wherefore God also hath highly exalted him, and given him a name which is above every name: **2:10** That at the name of Jesus every knee should bow, of things in heaven, and things in earth, and things under the earth; **2:11** And that every tongue should confess that Jesus Christ is Lord, to the glory of God the Father.

Therefore if we follow the example of Jesus Christ and are like-minded with him to love and obey God the Father in all things; God the Father will also raise us up in a resurrection to eternal life as a spirit, just as he raised up Jesus Christ to become the first of many like-minded resurrected to spirit brethren.

2:12 Wherefore, my beloved, as ye have always obeyed [God the Father], not as in my presence only, but now much more in my absence, work out your own salvation with fear and trembling.

Each and every person who has been personally and individually called to God the Father through Jesus Christ, is called to sincerely repent of sin, and to resolve to commit to sin no more: And if he does so he will have the sacrifice of Christ applied to himself in God's mercy.

We must work out our own salvation by faith in God's Word coupled with the works of faith, which are Abrahamic and Christ-like obedience to live by every Word of God the Father with passionate dedicated zeal (Mat 4:4).

If we are God's and have the Holy Spirit of God dwelling in us; then we will be doing the works and will of God the Father.

2:13 For it is God which worketh in you both to will and to do of his good pleasure.

Do not complain that a godly life is hard, and do avoid the sin of departing from a zeal to keep the whole Word of God to try and ease your life. Rather understand that God's ways are easy and that it is Satan's temptations and pressures which are designed to bring us back under his yoke which makes God's ways SEEM hard when they are not.

Remember the murmurings against God by Israel in the wilderness. Physical Israel did not understand and blamed God for their trials and sought to go back into the bondage of Egypt, instead of properly blaming the Adversary for their trials and crying out to God for deliverance.

Today spiritual Israel also tends to blame God for their trials, and instead of seeking deliverance from their Mighty One they seek to alleviate those trials by going their own ways; back into the bondage of compromise and sin: Which wickedness will bring strong correction from the Eternal.

When Satan and his influences are banished and all people are faithfully obeying God, life will be a paradise of peace, harmony and joy!

2:14 Do all things without murmurings and disputings: **2:15** That ye may be blameless and harmless, the sons of God, without rebuke, in the midst of a crooked and perverse nation, among whom ye shine as lights in the world;

If we are zealous for our Great God to learn and to live by every Word of God in passionate zeal, we shall be a Shining Light of example in a wicked world.

Those organizations that do their best to appear inoffensive and mainstream, seem completely ignorant of the fact that they appear as just another mainstream organization to those who see them.

To please God and to be a light of godly example; we must stand out in godliness, not blend in with the dark ignorance of worldliness.

The wicked, by following the foolishness of their own thoughts and doing the opposite of what God requires, think that they have found a recipe for success when they have really fallen away towards their own destruction

2:16 Holding forth the word of life [We like the Philippians are to follow, live by and stand on God's Word.]; that I may rejoice [when the brethren are resurrected to spirit] in the day of Christ, that I have not run [Godly teachers will rejoice that the Word of God has not been taught in vain, but that the brethren have profited by their admonitions to obey God.] in vain, neither laboured in vain.

Paul rejoices, as many others have done; in the sacrifices that they have made for their love of God and God's people

2:17 Yea, and if I be offered upon the sacrifice and service of your faith, I joy, and rejoice with you all. **2:18** For the same cause also do ye joy, and rejoice with me.

Paul will soon send Timothy who is like-minded with Paul in his love for the Philippians, to give them more news and instruction; and Timothy will then report back to Paul with the news from Philippi.

2:19 But I trust in the Lord Jesus to send Timotheus shortly unto you, that I also may be of good comfort, when I know your state. **2:20** For I have no man likeminded, who will naturally care for your state.

Paul laments that so many seek only their own advantage and do not seek to live by every Word of God; which is a common sin in today's spiritual Ekklesia.

2:21 For all seek their own, not the things which are Jesus Christ's.

Paul gives his approval of Timothy.

2:22 But ye know the proof of him, that, as a son with the father, he hath served with me in the gospel. **2:23** Him therefore I hope to send presently, so soon as I shall see how it will go with me.

Paul wants to come himself, but will first send those who can come immediately.

2:24 But I trust in the Lord that I also myself shall come shortly.

Epaphroditus was sent to Paul from Philippi to bring their tithes and gifts to Paul, and after his sickness Epaphroditus was sent back to Philippi to encourage the brethren there.

2:25 Yet I supposed it necessary to send to you Epaphroditus, my brother, and companion in labour, and fellowsoldier, but **your messenger, and he that ministered to my wants. 2:26** For he longed after you all, and was full of heaviness, because that ye had heard that he had been sick. **2:27** For indeed he was sick nigh unto death: but God had mercy on him; and not on him only, but on me also, lest I should have sorrow upon sorrow.

Paul was very careful to include Epaphroditus in his letter of encouragement to Philippi, and mentions to them that Epaphroditus had nearly died for the work of the gospel.

2:28 I sent him therefore the more carefully, that, when ye see him again, ye may rejoice, and that I may be the less sorrowful. **2:29** Receive him therefore in the Lord with all gladness; and hold such in reputation: **2:30 Because for the work of Christ he was nigh unto death, not regarding his life, to supply your lack of service toward me.**

Philippians 3

Philippians 3:1 Finally, my brethren, rejoice in the Lord. To write the same things to you, to me indeed is not grievous, but for you it is safe.

Paul repeatedly writes the same warnings to them and to us for our benefit throughout his epistles.

3:2 Beware of dogs [wolves (Mat 7:15), false shepherds], beware of evil workers [false teachers inside the assemblies], beware of the concision.

Watch out for unclean, unholy, idols of men which are wolves in sheep's clothing; who, though clever words deceive us away from any zeal for God to follow after themselves in order to devour us like vicious dogs [wolves], as Isaiah warned would be the case of the spiritual leaders and elders in these latter days.

> **Isaiah 56:10 His watchmen are blind: they are all ignorant, they are all dumb dogs** [wolves; false shepherds]**, they cannot bark** [give warning]**; sleeping, lying down, loving to slumber** [spiritually sleeping]**. 56:11 Yea, they are greedy dogs** [bad selfish shepherds, wolves ravaging the flock instead of shepherding it] **which can never have enough, and they are shepherds that cannot understand: they all look to their own way, every one for his gain, from his quarter.**

The faithful called out are circumcised in heart; they are diligent for God and they prove the words of men by the whole Word of God, trusting and having full confidence in God.

Philippians 3:3 For **we are the** [the true spiritually circumcised in heart Deu 10:16, 30:6] **circumcision, which worship God in the spirit, and rejoice in Christ Jesus, and have no confidence in the flesh.**

Paul then provides the credentials of his physical heritage and remarks that they are as nothing and were given up by Paul for Jesus Christ and the spiritual New Covenant of faith and the works of faith; which works of faith are wholehearted Christ-like obedience to God the Father in letter and in spirit.

3:4 Though I might also have confidence in the flesh. If any other man thinketh that he hath whereof he might trust in the flesh, I more: **3:5** Circumcised the eighth day, of the stock of Israel, of the tribe of Benjamin, an Hebrew of the Hebrews; as touching the law, a Pharisee; **3:6** Concerning zeal, persecuting the church; touching the righteousness which is in the law, blameless.

> When God rent the ten tribes of Israel away from Judah he left Benjamin with Judah, and Benjamin was to dwell with Judah forever, and in God's kingdom:
>
> > **Deuteronomy 33:12** And of Benjamin he said, The beloved of the Lord [Judah] shall dwell in safety by him; and the Lord shall cover him all the day long, and he shall dwell between his shoulders.
>
> After Messiah comes he will dwell between the shoulders [in the heart] of Benjamin.

The things that were to Paul's advantage in the flesh he cast aside as insignificant, to embrace the gospel of salvation through sincere repentance, the rejection of all sin, the application of the sacrifice of Christ and diligently living by every Word of God.

All those who believe being full of faith in the sinless life of Jesus Christ the Lamb of God and his resurrection to spirit by God the Father, and who reject all sin to live by every Word of God; will also raised up in a resurrection to eternal spirit.

3:7 But what things were gain to me, those I counted loss for Christ. **3:8** Yea doubtless, and I count all things but loss for the excellency of the knowledge of Christ Jesus my Lord: for whom I have suffered the loss of all things, and do count them but dung, that I may win Christ,

Righteousness does not come by keeping the law, for all have sinned and no amount of future law keeping can atone for PAST sin!

ONLY the sacrifice of Jesus Christ, which is only applied to the sincerely repentant who STOP sinning, can atone for PAST sin!

It is only by our faith and our works of faith to STOP sinning and the application of Christ's sacrifice, that we can be reconciled to God the Father and remain reconciled to him; and it is only by internalizing the whole Word of God [through studying and keeping it] that we may become holy as God is holy and righteous as God is righteous!

We must believe God and sincerely repent of all past sin to obey the Word of God in order to truly know God. Only when we have destroyed the old sinful self and become a new person in God through believing and living by every Word of God, can we be in the resurrection to spirit.

3:9 And be found in him, not having mine own righteousness, which is of the law, but that which is through the faith of Christ, the righteousness which is of God by faith: **3:10** That I may know him, and the power of his resurrection, and the fellowship of his sufferings, being made conformable unto his death; **3:11** If by any means I might attain unto the resurrection of the dead.

We must not think that we have already attained to godliness, but we are to continually grow in faith and knowledge; striving to root out all sin and striving to grow into the holiness and perfection of God the Father as defined by the Word and Will of God.

3:12 Not as though I had already attained, either were already perfect: but I follow after, if that I may apprehend that for which also I am apprehended of Christ Jesus.

We must also continually seek out growth in our understanding of the Word of God, and not reject advances in knowledge as most in the Ekklesia do today.

3:13 Brethren, I count not myself to have apprehended: but this one thing I do, forgetting those things which are behind, and reaching forth unto those things which are before, **3:14** I press toward the mark for the prize of the high calling of God in Christ Jesus.

3:15 Let us therefore, as many as [desire to be] be perfect, be thus minded: and if in any thing ye be otherwise minded, God shall reveal even this unto you.

If we are sincerely in error and desiring to be corrected, God's Spirit will lead us into all truth, if we diligently study all things to live by every Word of God.

Let us all be like-minded to be faithful to live by every Word of God and in complete unity with God alone; and to follow men ONLY as they faithfully follow the whole Word of God, taking note of and avoiding all deceitful men.

3:16 Nevertheless, whereto we have already attained, **let us walk by the same rule, let us mind the same thing. 3:17** Brethren, **be followers together of me, and mark them which walk so as ye have us for an ensample.**

Very many false teachers have crept into [of which we have had many warnings from the scriptures] today's spiritual Ekklesia, leading people astray from their zeal for God into a zeal for idols of men.

3:18 (For many walk, of whom I have told you often, and now tell you even weeping, that they are the enemies of the cross [enemies of the salvation of God by refusing to live by every Word of God] of Christ: **3:19** Whose end is destruction, whose God is their belly, and whose glory is in their shame, who mind earthly things.)

3:20 For our conversation [our conduct should be according to every Word of God] is in heaven; from whence also we look for the Saviour, the Lord Jesus Christ:

If we are diligent to faithfully destroy the old sinful person and to become a new person in Christ now; then we shall be changed to a glorious spiritual being in the resurrection to spirit.

3:21 Who shall change our vile body, that it may be fashioned like unto his glorious body, according to the working whereby he is able even to subdue all things unto himself.

Philippians 4

Paul concludes his letter to the Philippians by admonishing them to be of one mind in complete unity with Jesus Christ, who is of one mind in complete unity with God the Father.

Brethren, all this talk and desire to be united with men is a wrong priority and distraction from our calling to come into complete the unity with God the Father and Jesus Christ. It is time for us to wake up to the fact that we are called to be united with and to become like Jesus Christ and God the Father, and that any unity with men is to be based upon the foundation of unity with God the Father!

All those who are in complete unity with God the Father will also be in unity with one another, those who seek unity with men as their first priority will be distracted from unity with God!

Philippians 4:1 Therefore, my brethren dearly beloved and longed for, my joy and crown, so **stand fast in the Lord**, my dearly beloved.

4:2 I beseech Euodias, and beseech Syntyche, that they be of **the same mind in the Lord**. **4:3** And I intreat thee also, true yokefellow, help those women which laboured with me in the gospel, with Clement also, and with other my fellowlabourers, whose names are in the book of life.

Paul tells us to rejoice in the whole Word of God; which is the Gospel which defines the nature of God and reveals the way to salvation from bondage to sin and death, into eternal life.

4:4 Rejoice in the Lord alway: and again I say, Rejoice.

Be valiantly zealous for the whole Word of God, and be moderate in the things of the flesh.

4:5 Let your moderation be known unto all men. The Lord is at hand.

Do not be full of cares and concerns for worldly things, only make your needs known to God our Father who provides for our spiritual growth and salvation. Be passionate to follow our Mighty Deliverer to learn and to zealously live by every Word of God, to please God our Father and to be at peace with God always.

4:6 Be careful for nothing; but in every thing by prayer and supplication with thanksgiving let your requests be made known unto God. **4:7** And the peace of God, which passeth all understanding, shall keep your hearts and minds through Christ Jesus.

Cause our minds to dwell on positive things and to meditate day and night on the Word of God; and avoid dwelling on negative, sinful, and evil things.

4:8 Finally, brethren, **whatsoever things are true, whatsoever things are honest, whatsoever things are just, whatsoever things are pure, whatsoever things are lovely, whatsoever things are of good report; if there be any virtue, and if there be any praise, think on these things**.

Be ye doers of the Word; for if we marry the works of faith to our faith [belief], then we will be one in complete unity with God, and God will be at one with us.

4:9 Those things, which ye have both learned, and received, and heard, and seen in me [the scriptures written by Paul], **do: and the God of peace shall be with you.**

> **James 1:22** But be ye **doers of the word**, and not hearers only, deceiving your own selves.

Paul now rejoices, having realized that they had neglected him in the past because of lack of opportunity and had desired to help him.

Philippians 4:10 But I rejoiced in the Lord greatly, that now at the last your care of me hath flourished again; **wherein ye were also careful** [concerned], **but ye lacked opportunity**.

Paul has learned to be content with what he has and not to burn with desire for acquiring physical things; placing physical gain aside for joy to preach the gospel of salvation to all people.

4:11 Not that I speak in respect of want: for I have learned, in whatsoever state I am, therewith to be content. **4:12** I know both how to be abased, and I know how to abound: every where and in all things I am instructed [Paul had learned] both to be full and to be hungry, both to abound and to suffer need.

Paul thanks the Philippians who had evidently communicated with him when they had learned of his need.

4:13 I can do all things through Christ which strengtheneth me. **4:14** Notwithstanding ye have well done, that ye did communicate with my affliction.

It was often the Philippians only, who sent help to Paul for his needs.

4:15 Now ye Philippians know also, that in the beginning of the gospel, when I departed from Macedonia, no church communicated with me as concerning giving and receiving, but ye only. **4:16** For even in Thessalonica ye sent once and again unto my necessity.

Paul delights in the gifts that the Philippians had sent him, but delights even more that they are full of love and concern for him and for what he has preached to them.

4:17 Not because I desire a gift: but I desire fruit that may abound to your account. **4:18** But I have all, and abound: I am full, having received of Epaphroditus the things which were sent from you, an odour of a sweet smell, a sacrifice acceptable, wellpleasing to God.

Paul then prays that God will supply all of their needs, just as they have supplied his needs; and Paul glorifies God the Father.

4:19 But my God shall supply all your need according to his riches in glory by Christ Jesus. **4:20** Now **unto God and our Father be glory for ever and ever**. Amen.

Paul salutes every person who is in Christ and is full of faithful Christ-like zeal to serve God the Father.

4:21 Salute every saint in Christ Jesus. The brethren which are with me greet you.

This letter to the Philippians, written from Rome, includes greetings from all the saints living at Rome to all the saints living at Philippi; and indicates that there were saints even in the household of the emperor himself!

4:22 All the saints salute you, chiefly they that are of Caesar's household.

4:23 The grace [May the mercy of God the Father and Jesus Christ be poured out on all sincerely repentant persons who are passionate to live by every Word of God!] of our Lord Jesus Christ be with you all. Amen.

Colossians

Colossians 1

The Book of Colossians was written to the brethren at Colossae and to the brethren of Laodicea; it is therefore a direct message to today's spiritual Ekklesia; who are for the most part latter day Laodiceans.

Paul was the apostle to the Gentiles and everywhere he went he spoke first to the Jews and was usually rejected by most of them and then went to speak to the Gentiles.

Paul greets those who are faithful to follow God the Father and Jesus Christ

Colossians 1:1 Paul, an apostle of Jesus Christ by the will of God, and Timotheus our brother, **1:2** To the saints and faithful brethren in Christ which are at Colosse: Grace [mercy] be unto you, and peace, from God our Father and the Lord Jesus Christ.

Paul pronounces a blessing of forgiveness and peace with God because of their sincere repentance and dedicated love of God and love of keeping God's Word; then he lets them know that he and his companions are praying for them.

Even so, God the Father and Jesus Christ love us and are ready to forgive and to feed us with the Word of God (Rev 3:20), if we will only abandon our idols of men and false traditions and dedicate ourselves to a passionate wholehearted love to live by every Word of God.

1:3 We give thanks to God and the Father of our Lord Jesus Christ, praying always for you, **1:4** Since we heard of your faith [and works of faith] in Christ Jesus, and of the love which ye have to all the saints,

Paul points out that they have been faithful to the truth of the way to salvation that was preached to them, and mentions that they will receive a rich spiritual reward for their diligence to learn godliness. They are informed that Paul knows of their diligence because Epaphras has reported to Paul of their zeal and faithfulness to God.

This is prophetic of a yet future repentance and zeal for godliness in today's Ekklesia once we have been corrected in the furnace of tribulation.

1:5 For the hope [reward of eternal life] which is laid up for you in heaven, whereof ye heard before in the word of the truth of the gospel; **1:6** Which is come unto you, as it is in all the world; and bringeth forth fruit, as it doth also in you, since the day ye heard of it, and knew the grace [mercy] of God in truth: **1:7** As ye also learned of **Epaphras our dear fellowservant, who is for you a faithful minister of Christ; 1:8 Who also declared unto us your love in the Spirit.**

Paul and his companions pray for the spiritual growth of God's true called out; that they may be filled with the whole Word of God, and strengthened by God's Spirit.

1:9 For this cause we also, since the day we heard it, do not cease to pray for you, and to **desire that ye might be filled with the knowledge of his will in all wisdom and spiritual understanding; 1:10 That ye might walk worthy of the Lord** [living by every Word of God] **unto all pleasing, being fruitful in every good work** [keeping the whole Word of God]**, and increasing in the knowledge of God; 1:11 Strengthened with all might, according to his glorious power, unto all patience and longsuffering with joyfulness**;

Paul now begins to get into doctrine

1:12 Giving thanks unto the Father, which hath made us meet [called us and delivered us] to be partakers of the inheritance of the saints in light: **1:13** Who hath delivered us from the power of darkness, and **hath translated us into the kingdom of his dear Son:**

Those who are zealous for the keeping of God's Word are actually being zealous to keep the constitution and laws of God's Kingdom. Although that Kingdom has not yet come to rule over the earth, in a spiritual sense the faithful are internalizing the nature of the Head of that kingdom, God the Father.

1:14 In whom [Jesus Christ] we have redemption through his blood [sacrifice], even the forgiveness of [sincerely repented PAST] sins:

Paul proclaims that before he ave up his godhood to be made flesh, Jesus Christ was the Creator and is a member of the family of God, and that Jesus Christ is the HEAD of the true spiritual Ekklesia under God the Father.

1:15 Who is the image of the invisible God, the firstborn of every creature: **1:16 For by him were all things created, that are in heaven, and that are in earth, visible and invisible, whether they be thrones, or dominions, or principalities, or powers: all things were created by him, and for him: 1:17 And he is before all things, and by him all things consist. 1:18 And he is the head of the body, the church: who is the beginning, the firstborn from the dead; that in all things he** [Jesus Christ is preeminent over all; under God the Father.] **might have the preeminence.**

1:19 for it pleased the Father that in him should all fulness dwell; **1:20** And, having made peace through the blood of his cross [The application of Christ's sacrificial death brings peace between people and God.], by him to reconcile all things unto himself [God the Father]; by him [by Christ], I say, whether they be things in earth, or things in heaven.

Jesus Christ has atoned for all sincerely repented PAST sins, and has reconciled the repentant who commit to sin no more and to live by every Word of God; to God the Father.

1:21 And you, that were sometime alienated and enemies in your mind by wicked works, yet now hath he [Christ] reconciled [the sincerely repentant to God the Father]

Jesus Christ the Creator God, gave up his Godhood to be made flesh, and then he gave up his physical life in the flesh to die and atone for all who will stop sinning and turn to live by every Word of God. If we therefore endure and continue in zealously keeping the whole Word of God without any compromise or any hint of turning aside; we will be resurrected to spirit just as Jesus Christ was resurrected back to spirit!

1:22 In the body of his flesh through death, to [Christ died so that he could present us blameless before God the Father, though Christ's sacrifice], **present you holy and unblameable and unreproveable in his sight:**

1:23 If ye continue in the faith [and the works of faith; which is living by every Word of God] grounded and settled [on the sound doctrine of the whole Word of God; the apostles and prophets who wrote the scripture], and be not moved away from the hope of the gospel [Let us not be moved away from any part of the whole Word of God, which is the way of salvation and life eternal.], which ye have heard, and which was preached to every creature which is under heaven; whereof I Paul am made a minister;

Jesus, Paul and all of God's servants, endured and endure persecutions and afflictions so that they may rejoice over the deliverance of humanity.

1:24 Who now rejoice in my sufferings for you, and fill up that which is behind of the afflictions of Christ in my flesh for his [Christ's] body's sake, which is the church [the faithful brethren]: **1:25** Whereof I am made a minister, according to the dispensation of God which is given to me for you, to fulfil the word of God;

The mystery of the plan of God for the salvation of man, both Jew and Gentile, is contained in the scriptures, and has been made known to those truly called to God who faithfully live by every Word of God.

1:26 Even **the mystery which hath been hid from ages and from generations, but now is made manifest to his saints**:

The mystery of the ages is the sacrificial death of the Lamb of God for the sins of the world, AND that God will dwell in each of his people through the agency of the Holy Spirit; empowering and enabling them to live by every Word of God just as Jesus Christ did: Enabling those who follow God's Spirit with a passionate love of the truth, to overcome and endure to the end, just as Jesus Christ overcame all sin and was blameless before God the Father!

1:27 To whom God would make known what is the riches of the glory of this mystery among the Gentiles; **which is Christ in you, the hope of glory**: **1:28** Whom we preach, warning every man, and teaching every man in all wisdom; that we may present every man perfect in Christ Jesus: **1:29** Whereunto I also labour, striving according to his working, which worketh in me mightily.

We sinned through the breaking of God the Father's Word which is living contrary to the nature and Spirit of God. We are reconciled to God by sincere repentance, a commitment to STOP sinning, and the application of the sacrifice of Christ, and then being washed clean by learning and keeping the whole Word of God.

Why then would we go back into the spiritual Egypt of bondage to sin and offense against the nature and Spirit of God the Father, in the name of some false fantasy of our own imaginations about the nature of love, the nature of God [for God IS love]; doing what we think is right, instead of doing what God says is right?

Yes, the ways of God are the ways of love: and those ways, that love; is defined by the Law and Word of God. Therefore any compromise with any part of the Word of God is a compromise with the love and nature of God!

Watch out for the heresy which teaches tolerance for lawlessness in the name of a false concept of love [Jude], or in the name of organizational unity. Our unity is to be complete unity and oneness with God the Father, just as Jesus Christ was united with God the Father in every way.

Jesus Christ did NOT sacrifice his unity with God the Father for organizational unity with the religious establishment of his day: and neither should we!

Jesus Christ kept all of his Father's Word in both letter and spirit, WITHOUT COMPROMISE: If WE are to be like Christ and God the Father; we MUST do likewise!

Sincere repentance and the application of the sacrificial death of the physical Jesus Christ atones for our PAST sincerely repented sins, and a commitment to STOP sinning in future, purifies us so that we can be presented to God the Father holy and blameless and beyond reproach in his sight: and IF we remain in a faithful relationship with God through a passionate love that reveals itself in our zeal for all that pertains to him, including diligently living by every Word of God.

Yet, if we turn back into bondage to sin and compromise with the Will and Word of God the Father, we shall indeed be rebuked, just as those who wanted to turn back into Egypt were destroyed from before the Eternal in the wilderness.

In order to inherit eternal life we must STOP sinning and we must continue in the ways of God, never departing from them nor compromising with them, even to the point of suffering and death.

Colossians 2

Colossians 2:1 For I would that ye knew what great conflict [deep concern] I have for you, **and for them at Laodicea, and for as many as have not seen my face in the flesh**; **2:2** That their hearts might be comforted, being knit together in love [Godly love is living by every Word of God.], and unto all riches of the full assurance of understanding [of the Word of God, to the acknowledgement of the mystery of God [the plan of salvation], and of the Father, and of Christ; **2:3** In whom are hid all the treasures of wisdom and knowledge.

The whole Word of God is the wisdom and knowledge of God. Let no one beguile us into sin and compromise with any part of the whole Word of God.

2:4 And this I say, lest any man should beguile you with enticing words.

Just as Paul was absent from Colossae at that time, he is also absent in the flesh from us today; but we have his written scriptural admonitions that we should be always zealous to live by every Word and the Will of God.

2:5 For though I be absent in the flesh, yet am I with you in the spirit, joying and beholding your order [orderliness in pursuing godliness], and the stedfastness of your faith [and the works of faith which is the diligent keeping of every Word of God] in Christ.

If we have sincerely repented and made a baptismal commitment to sin no more; we will receive the gift of the Holy Spirit and we are to live as Christ lived, through the strength of Jesus Christ living in us.

2:6 As ye have therefore received Christ Jesus the Lord, so **walk ye in him**: **2:7 Rooted and built up in him, and stablished in the faith, as ye have been taught, abounding therein with thanksgiving.**

> **1 John 2:6** He that saith he abideth in him ought himself also so to walk [live], even as he walked [lived and lives].

Stay fully grounded on the sound doctrine of Every Word of God and let no person deceive you into compromising with any part of the whole Word of God.

Contend earnestly for the Scriptures as admonished by Jude and never compromise with the Sabbath or any part of the Word of God. Jesus will never blink at a little willful sin, he will cast the sinner out of God the Father's Temple! We should love God the Father and Jesus Christ so much that any willful sin would be disgustingly repellent to us.

Let no one spoil [plunder and gain control over us] us by enticing us to cook, travel or buy food or anything else on God's Sabbath and Holy Days, or lead us into minimizing and compromising with any part of the Word of God.

Let no one entice us to reject God's Biblical Calendar for the apostate Rabbinic Calendar and let no man entice us to tolerate any sin; and do prove all things by the Holy Scriptures.

Beware of those who use the name of Christ to falsely teach us to tolerate sin, saying that because Christ died for us we no longer need to be zealous to live by every Word of God.

Colossians 2:8 Beware lest any man spoil [make plunder of you, and overcome you] **you through philosophy** [clever arguments] **and vain deceit** [false teachings]**, after the tradition of men, after the rudiments of the world, and not after Christ.**

2:9 For in him [Jesus Christ] dwelleth all the fulness of the Godhead bodily.

We are spiritually circumcised with the removal of our PAST sins and the old sinful man was destroyed in the watery grave of baptism; so that we may rise up new people in Christ, being passionate to live by every Word of God in Christ-like zeal.

Then, IF we are diligent to learn, to grow and to overcome through the power of Christ dwelling in us by the Holy Spirit; we shall be raised up from the grave incorruptible, just as Jesus Christ was raised up incorruptible.

2:10 And ye are complete in him, which is the head of all principality and power: **2:11** In whom also **ye are circumcised with the circumcision made without hands, in putting off the body of the sins of the flesh by the circumcision of Christ: 2:12 Buried with him in baptism, wherein also ye are risen with him through the faith of the operation of God, who hath raised him from the dead.**

We the wicked, have been reconciled to God the Father and cleansed of our PAST sins, by sincere repentance and the application of the atoning sacrifice of Jesus Christ, if we commit to go forward and sin no more.

We, who faced eternal death for our sins, have been saved to a resurrection to eternal life by the mercy of God the Father and Jesus Christ.

2:13 And you, being dead in your sins and the uncircumcision [unconverted wickedness] of your flesh, hath he [the Father] quickened [makes spiritually alive] together with him [Christ], having forgiven you all trespasses [through our sincere repentance, commitment to STOP sinning and the application of the sacrifice of Christ];

God the Father erased the indictment against us; He erased the list of our past sins because of our sincere repentance and the application of the sacrifice of Christ.

In no way does Christ's sacrifice do away with the law of sacrifice, rather it fulfills that law; by offering a PERFECT sacrifice for sincerely repented PAST sins; obligating us to go forward and sin no more.

If we seek the application of Christ's sacrifice and then continue in sin, we make a mockery of that sacrifice and we have not truly repented at all.

> **Hebrews 10:26** For if we sin wilfully after that we have received the knowledge of the truth, there remaineth no more sacrifice for sins, **10:27** But a certain fearful looking for of judgment and fiery indignation, which shall devour the adversaries.
>
> **10:28** He that despised Moses' law died without mercy under two or three witnesses: **10:29** Of how much sorer [greater] punishment,

suppose ye, shall he be thought worthy, who hath trodden under foot the Son of God [by continuing in sin], and hath counted the blood of the [the sacrifice of the New Covenant, Jesus Christ the Lamb of God] covenant, wherewith he was sanctified, an unholy thing [asking for its application without real repentance], and hath done despite [is contemptuous of Christ's sacrifice and God's mercy, by continuing in sin] unto the Spirit of grace?

Colossians 2:14 Blotting out the handwriting of ordinances that was against us, which was contrary to us, and took it out of the way, nailing it to his cross;

The ordinances which were against us was the indictment - the list of our sins for which we faced eternal death; which list of crimes is paid in full by our sincere repentance, a commitment to STOP sinning and the application the sacrifice of the Lamb of God to us. The list of our sins, the indictment against us; was paid in full by the application of the death of Christ to the sincerely repentant.

Jesus Christ through his perfect sinless life and his willingness to obey God the Father to the death, was worthy to be given all power in the universe [under God the Father]

2:15 And having spoiled principalities and powers, he made a shew of them openly, triumphing over them in it.

Therefore we are to keep God's Sabbaths, New Moons and Holy Days, we may eat scripturally clean meats and we are to be diligent to avoid unclean things; which teaches us to put a difference between the holy and the profane.

We are to live by all things which are written in the Word of God, and we are not to permit any person to criticize us and turn us away from living by every Word of God.

The reference to meat and drink is a direct reference to the asceticism, vegetarianism and teetotaler teachings of the Stoics, as traditions of men which might appear humble but are really self-willed.

True humility is faithfulness to submit to and live by every Word of God in deeds [the works of faith] and not mere appearances.

Every Word of God is commanded to be kept, and without living by every Word of God, we cannot understand spiritual things.

This is why there is so little understanding today, because we do not keep the Sabbath, Holy Days and New Moons on the dates proscribed by the Word of God, and we do not keep them in the way that God's Word commands.

2:16 Let no man therefore judge you in meat, or in drink, or in respect of an holyday, or of the new moon, or of the sabbath days: 2:17 Which are a shadow of things to come; but the body [the complete scriptures, including these things, define the nature of Jesus Christ and God the Father] **is of Christ.**

Let no person deceive you with a mere appearance of humility while really being full of pride, teaching their own errors and teaching to keep the false traditions of men instead of exalting the Head of the body, God the Father and Jesus Christ.

2:18 Let no man beguile you of your reward in a voluntary humility [with a mere appearance of humility] and worshipping of angels [Worshiping is obeying and exalting spirits, messengers, pastors, teachers or anything above God.], intruding into those things which he hath not seen [teaching error contrary to the scriptures], vainly puffed up by his fleshly mind [full of pride and their own false ways],

We must let no man or even a spirit beguile us away from living by every Word of God, no matter how humble or wise they appear to be or what title they claim. An apostle or prophet who exalts himself is a false apostle or false prophet.

2:19 And not holding the Head [Not exalting God the Father and Jesus Christ, but using the name of Christ to lead people away from Christ to follow after themselves and their own false traditions and false ways (Mat 24).], from which all the body by joints and bands having nourishment [Spiritual food, the Bread of Life, the whole Word of God] ministered, and knit together [with God and Christ], increaseth with the increase of God.

We produce godly fruit as we increase in the knowledge of God and the works of faith, there is No spiritual value in following men or spirits contrary to the Word of God.

If the PAST sinful person is now dead to sin, why do we still desire to follow worldly things? This is speaking of the teachings of men which appear humanly humble and wise but are not consistent with the Word of God.

2:20 Wherefore if ye be dead with Christ from the rudiments of the world, why, as though living in the world, are ye subject to ordinances, **2:21** (Touch not; taste not; handle not; **2:22** Which all are to perish with the using;) **after the commandments and doctrines of men? 2:23** Which things have indeed a shew of wisdom in will worship, and humility, and neglecting of the body: not in any honour to the satisfying of the flesh.

Do not worship, do not follow and obey any man or spirit who teaches us to break or to compromise with any part of the Word of God. Do not let anyone beguile you or entice you to follow them and the false contrary to scripture traditions of men, by putting on a show of supposed humility and using clever arguments.

> **2 Corinthians 11:14** And no marvel; for Satan himself is transformed into an angel of light. **11:15** Therefore it is no great thing if his ministers also be transformed as the ministers of righteousness; whose end shall be according to their works.

Do not let anyone entice you into following men or spirits by the clever arguments of men which are not the sound doctrine of the scriptures.

Do not be deceived by people who are trying to deceive you with clever reasoning's about things which they do not understand themselves.

Do not be deceived by people who are putting up a pretense of humility and godliness to impress, while teaching contrary to the Word of God.

Do not let these puffed up charlatans, who may APPEAR humble; entice you into sinning against God, by leading you into compromising with any part of the Word of God.

These seducers, these false teachers; do not hold Jesus Christ as their Head under his Head, God the Father; but rather they try to be the mediator between men and God themselves. They try to come between the people and God and they try to be the Head themselves in the eyes of the people. They USE the name of Christ to deceive people away from the doctrines of Christ.

How can we resist this effort to steal our crowns and the birthright of our calling?

Satan tries to confuse the issues while they are actually very simple. All kingdoms are based on a constitution and a set of laws. Always keep God's Word and do all of God's Will zealously, out of a passionate love for God the Father and his Word, without any hint of compromise.

The whole Word of God is the foundation that NO man can ever shake.

False teachers try to appear like some great, humble and Godly person, so that they can entice you and distract you away from the doctrines of God the Father and Jesus Christ.

If we stand on the Word of God, the will of God, the things of God; then we have a strong unshakable defense against the false doctrines and false traditions of men.

Colossians 3

Colossians 3:1 If ye then be risen [risen from the waters of baptism into godliness] with Christ, seek those things which are above [seek godly things and not worldliness], where Christ sitteth on the right hand of God [the Father]. **3:2** Set your affection on things above, not on things on the earth [seek spiritual things and not fixate on physical things]. **3:3** For ye [our PAST sinful person is dead in repentance and baptism] are dead, and your life is hid [the sincerely repentant baptized person is to become a new being at one in full unity with God] with Christ in God.

Our new life is to be a Christ-like life so that when he comes we may be changed to a glorified spirit body and live forever through the sacrifice and salvation of Christ and the mercy of God the Father.

3:4 When Christ, who is our life [The application of the sacrifice of Jesus Christ gives us eternal life if we are faithful to STOP sinning.], shall appear, then shall ye also appear [be resurrected to be with him] with him in glory.

3:5 Mortify [kill, destroy] therefore your [We must destroy our PAST wicked person, and STOP sinning and living contrary to any part of the whole Word of God.] members which are upon the earth; fornication, uncleanness, inordinate affection [unlawful affections], evil concupiscence [mentally fantasizing about doing wickedness and evil], and covetousness [placing our personal desires above God's Word], which is idolatry: **3:6 For which things' sake the wrath of God cometh on the children of disobedience:**

Today the spiritual Ekklesia are children of disobedience to God, being FULL of idolatry and spiritual adultery as they make idols of men and false traditions; breaking God's Word to please men.

We are supposed to have sincerely repented of our idolatry and wickedness, and instead we have gone back into spiritual adultery by loving men and false traditions more than we love God; and following men instead of proving men and being zealous to learn and live by every Word of God.

Just like the Mosaic Pharisees, today's spiritual Ekklesia teaches the doctrines of men and follows idols of men, contrary to the Word of God.

Today the Sabbath and High Days are called holy and then continually polluted, and in very many other things we defy God's Word to follow the doctrines [teachings] of men.

> **Matthew 15:7** Ye hypocrites, well did Esaias prophesy of you, saying,
>
> **15:8** This people draweth nigh unto me with their mouth, and honoureth me with their lips; but their heart is far from me.
>
> **15:9** But **in vain they do worship me, teaching for doctrines the commandments of men.**

Colossians 3:7 In the which [We have all sinned in the past, yet we are now supposed to have repented and to have STOPPED sinning.] ye also walked some time, when ye lived in them.

3:8 But now ye also put off all these; anger, wrath, malice, blasphemy, filthy communication [Filthy communication is far more than gutter talk, and includes any false teaching that leads us away from our zeal to live by every Word of God.] out of your mouth.

3:9 Lie not one to another [do not teach any false thing], seeing that ye have put off the old man [we are to repent and put off the sin in our past] with his deeds;

3:10 And have put on the new man [We are to become a new person with Christ dwelling is us, so that we may be godly just as Jesus Christ was and is godly.], which is renewed in knowledge [knowledge of godliness and the whole Word of God through the Spirit of Christ dwelling in us] after the image of him [Christ] that created him [us]:

All those who are one in mind and spirit with God the Father and Jesus Christ; are a new and holy people, made one in Jesus Christ and those who are in full unity with God are not many peoples, but have become ONE nation and one godly people!

> **1 Peter 2:9** But ye are a chosen generation, a royal priesthood, an holy nation, a peculiar people; that ye should shew forth the praises [be a Shining Light of godly example] of him who hath called you out of darkness into his marvellous light;

Colossians 3:11 Where there is neither Greek nor Jew, circumcision nor uncircumcision, Barbarian, Scythian, bond nor free: but Christ is all, and in all.

Godly people are to put away all wickedness and are to live just as Christ lived; being bold and strong to warn and to rebuke all sin just as Jesus Christ and Paul did, and being quick to forgive even those who had hated and persecuted us.

3:12 Put on therefore, as the elect of God, holy and beloved, bowels of mercies, kindness, humbleness of mind, meekness, longsuffering; **3:13** Forbearing one another, and forgiving one another, if any man have a quarrel against any: even as Christ forgave you, so also do ye. **3:14** And above all these things put on charity [Godly love, which is defined by the law of God], which is the bond of perfectness.

> **2 John 1:6** And **this is love**, that we walk after his commandments.

> **1 John 5:3** For **this is the love of God**, that we keep his commandments: and his commandments are not grievous.

We are to be at peace with God through living by ALL of God's Word, doing God's Will and doing all those things that please our heavenly Father and our eternal Husband and High Priest, Jesus Christ; and by being at peace with God in this way, the peace of God [the Word of God] will dwell in our hearts.

> **Jeremiah 31:33** But this shall be the covenant that I will make with the house of Israel; After those days, saith the Lord, **I will put my law in their inward parts, and write it in their hearts; and will be their God, and they shall be my people.**

When our hearts are full of God, we will be continually thinking on godly things and we will bubble over with joy and singing about God and our love for God.

Colossians 3:15 And let the peace of God rule in your hearts, to the which also ye are called in one body; and be ye thankful. **3:16 Let the word of Christ dwell in you richly in all wisdom; teaching and admonishing one another in psalms and hymns and spiritual songs, singing with grace in your hearts to the Lord.**

All that we do, should be consistent with every Word of God, and should be a Shining Light of godly example for all to see.

3:17 And whatsoever ye do in word or deed, do all in the name of the Lord Jesus, giving thanks to God and the Father by him.

Some instructions in godliness: Wives are to submit to their husbands as an example that we are all to submit to our spirit Husband Jesus Christ. Husbands are never to bully their wives but to love them and give themselves for them, just as Christ lived for and gave his life for his bride.

3:18 Wives, submit yourselves unto your own husbands, as it is fit in the Lord. **3:19** Husbands, love your wives, and be not bitter against them.

Children are to obey their parents in the Lord, because we are all the children of God and we are all to obey God our Father in heaven for our own good. Parents are to lead their children wisely, teaching them godliness by word, deed and by example, only disciplining only after much patient guidance, treating our own children just as our heavenly Father treats us.

3:20 Children, obey your parents in all things: for this is well pleasing unto the Lord. **3:21** Fathers, provoke not your children to anger, lest they be discouraged.

Obey God first and then obey those in authority over us; honestly, wholeheartedly; and not with mere lip service and eye service.

3:22 Servants, obey in all things your masters according to the flesh; not with eyeservice, as menpleasers; but in singleness of heart, fearing God; **3:23** And **whatsoever ye do, do it heartily, as to the Lord, and not unto men**; **3:24** Knowing that of the Lord ye shall receive the reward of the inheritance: for ye serve the Lord Christ.

Those who do well will receive their reward; and those who sin willfully will receive their correction, and if unrepentant they will go to destruction.

3:25 But he that doeth wrong shall receive for the wrong which he hath done: and there is no respect of persons.

Colossians 4

Pay what you honestly owe others, before making offerings or spending extravagantly, and pay your servants [hired help] promptly.

Yes we are to give what is lawfully requires but it is a SIN to give large offerings when your family is in desperate need or when you have unpaid debts to go home to.

> **Mark 7:9** And he said unto them, Full well ye reject the commandment of God, that ye may keep your own tradition.
>
> **7:10** For Moses said, Honour thy father and thy mother; and, Whoso curseth father or mother, let him die the death:
>
> **7:11** But ye say, If a man shall say to his father or mother, It is Corban, that is to say, a gift, [an offering] by whatsoever thou mightest be profited by me; he shall be free.
>
> **7:12** And ye suffer [permit him to give the offering and neglect his family] him no more to do ought for his father or his mother;
>
> **7:13** Making the word of God of none effect through your tradition, which ye have delivered: and many such like things do ye.

Brethren, such wickedness abounds in today's spiritually called out Ekklesia: We give and give to our corporate entities while neglecting our responsibilities to our families and our debtors. This is a great SIN in the brotherhood!

> **1 Timothy 5:8** But if any provide not for his own, and specially for those of his own house, he hath denied the faith, and is worse than an infidel.

Colossians 4:1 Masters, give unto your servants that which is just and equal; knowing that ye also have a Master in heaven.

Pray and be in constant mental contact with God by thinking on the things of God.

4:2 Continue in prayer, and watch in the same with thanksgiving;

I echo Paul in also asking for your prayers for me and this work.

4:3 Withal praying also for us, that God would open unto us a door of utterance, to speak the mystery of Christ, for which I am also in bonds: **4:4** That I may make it manifest, as I ought to speak.

Be careful how you relate with those who lack the light that guides us; maintain your godliness and give an answer to their questions, but do not engage in pointless strife.

4:5 Walk in wisdom toward them that are without, redeeming the time. **4:6** Let your speech be alway with grace, seasoned with salt, that ye may know how ye ought to answer every man.

The message is being sent by Tychicus, and Onesimus who also carried the letter to Philemon.

4:7 All my state shall Tychicus declare unto you, who is a beloved brother, and a faithful minister and fellowservant in the Lord: **4:8** Whom I have sent unto you for the same purpose, that he might know your estate, and comfort your hearts; **4:9** With Onesimus, a faithful and beloved brother, who is one of you. They shall make known unto you all things which are done here.

4:10 Aristarchus my fellowprisoner [in Rome] saluteth you, and Marcus, sister's son to Barnabas, (touching whom ye received commandments: if he come unto you, receive him;) **4:11** And Jesus, which is called Justus, who are of the circumcision. These only are my fellowworkers unto the kingdom of God, which have been a comfort unto me.

4:12 Epaphras, who is one of you, a servant of Christ, saluteth you, always labouring fervently for you in prayers, that ye may stand perfect and complete in all the will of God. **4:13** For I bear him record, that he hath a great zeal for you, and them that are in Laodicea, and them in Hierapolis.

4:14 Luke, the beloved physician, and Demas, greet you.

4:15 Salute the brethren which are in Laodicea, and Nymphas, and the church which is in his house. **4:16** And **when this epistle is read among you, cause that it be read also in the church of the Laodiceans;** and that ye likewise read the epistle from Laodicea.

4:17 And say to Archippus, Take heed to the ministry which thou hast received in the Lord, that thou fulfil it.

4:18 The salutation by the hand of me Paul. Remember my bonds. Grace be with you; Amen.

First Thessalonians

1 Thessalonians 1

The epistles to the Thessalonians were recorded and preserved for God's faithful pillars, who stand unshakable on every Word of God; encouraging them in their patient enduring while giving them key prophetic information.

While the epistles of Paul are addressed to individual congregations; they are likewise preserved as Holy Scripture and recorded for the instruction of all those who are called by God.

1 Thessalonians 1:1 Paul, and Silvanus, and Timotheus, unto the church of the Thessalonians which is in [faithfully obeying] God the Father and in the Lord Jesus Christ: Grace be unto you, and peace, from God our Father, and the Lord Jesus Christ.

Just as Colossians was meant as an encouragement to godliness for the Colossians and the latter day Laodiceans, this epistle is especially for the faithful pillars in Thessaloniki and for the faithful pillars throughout history and in these later days.

The Thessalonians were full of faith and the works of faith, and they were diligent to patiently live by every Word of God and so are the spiritual pillars of these last days and of all ages. We are to patiently endure, growing in godliness and overcoming all sin, and in so doing we shall be saved at the resurrection to spirit.

> **Luke 21:19** In your patience possess ye your souls [attain eternal life].

Colossians was written specifically to Laodicea (Rev 3:14-22) and the epistles to the Thessalonians were (and are) a direct encouragement and instruction for the pillars, called the Philadelphian Ekklesia in Revelation 3.

1 Thessalonians 1:2 We give thanks to God always for you all, making mention of you in our prayers; **1:3** Remembering without ceasing **your work of faith, and labour of love, and patience of hope in our Lord Jesus Christ, in the sight of God and our Father; 1:4** Knowing, brethren beloved, your election [calling] of God.

This letter is addressed to the Thessalonians who are presented as faithful pillars of light.

These messages contain no correction at all, only instructions and encouragement for God's pillars. Those folks in Thessaloniki had a true Philadelphian attitude of love for and of living by every Word of God; which is emulated by God's faithful pillars throughout the ages.

1:5 For our gospel came not unto you in word only, but also in power, and in the Holy Ghost, and in much assurance; as ye know what manner of men we were among you for your sake.

The pillars are called out with much affliction and endure very much for God's way, yet they remain solidly grounded on the sound doctrine of the whole Word of God. They follow every Word of God with joy and through their zeal for all things of God, are full of the Holy Spirit of TRUTH.

1:6 And ye became followers of us, and of the Lord, having received the word in much affliction, with joy of the Holy Ghost.

Paul reminds them that they received the Word of God through much affliction; meaning that they suffered much for the sake of their love, zeal and faith toward God.

The pillars know that they were sinners and they know that they are weak, and that they are saved by the mercy and power of God. Therefore they stand upon and rely upon their Mighty Deliverer, cleaving to him and continually relying upon their Mighty One; diligently living by every

Word of God and never turning aside to follow idols of men or their own imaginations.

They endure adversity and receive and embrace the truth of God with great joy.

Where has that great joy in discovering and understanding the things of God gone in the Laodicean church of today? Has it not been buried in a misguided zeal for false traditions and idols of men, instead of a Philadelphian love of the TRUTH?

True spiritual pillars are a Shining Light of example for their Laodicean brethren who reject them for a time; but will later remember that shining example and likewise turn to the Eternal!

1:7 So that ye were ensamples to all that believe in Macedonia and Achaia.

Today the spiritual Ekklesia has fallen far away from a godly zeal and Philadelphian love for TRUTH and an enthusiastic zeal for all of God's Word; falling into a blind unquestioning faith in idols of men above their first love and faith in our espoused Husband and his Father.

How did this happen?

They were deceived by thinking that "Philadelphia" means brotherly love [love for men] while forgetting that the proper foundation of brotherly love is passionate love for God the Father.

All those who love God the Father and live by every Word of God will be bound together by their mutual love of God and will love one another on that common foundation. That is the definition of a Philadelphian pillar!

True Philadelphian love is to love God with all our beings, and if we truly love God we will seek to please him and we will do what God teaches us. Our love of God and our living by every Word of God then becomes the foundation for loving mankind.

> **Matthew 22:37** Jesus said unto him, Thou shalt love the Lord thy God with all thy heart, and with all thy soul, and with all thy mind. **22: 38 This is the first and great commandment. 22:39** And the second is like unto it, Thou shalt love thy neighbour as thyself.

If God is left out of the equation by paying lip service to God but having no love to live by every Word of God the Father; our love of people becomes idolatry because it exalts love for people above love for God.

Yet today, there are still a few faithful pillars like those Thessalonians, and the scattered Philadelphian pillars are a Shining Light of passionate zeal to live by every Word of God.

1 Thessalonians 1:8 For from you sounded out the word of the Lord not only in Macedonia and Achaia, but also **in every place your faith to Godward is spread abroad**; so that we need not to speak any thing.

Others will one day point to the example of the faithfulness and zeal of the patiently enduring pillars; and how we turned from idolizing men to serve the Omnipotent Almighty God.

1:9 For they themselves [others will see our example] shew of us what manner of entering in we had unto you, and how **ye turned to God from idols to serve the living and true God; 1:10** And to wait [to wait patiently for the deliverance of the coming Christ] for his Son from heaven, whom he raised from the dead, even Jesus, which delivered us from the wrath to come.

The Thessalonians and the faithful pillars have always received the Word of Truth with joy, and have cleaved to the Word of the Eternal God through the strength of his Spirit; which is given to those who love and live by every Word of God.

1 Thessalonians 2

Paul, even after his previous experiences of persecution, was bold to preach the truth to the Thessalonians against much opposition. Today the truth of God is preached even in the professing spiritual Ekklesia, only through much opposition from the very corporate assemblies themselves.

1 Thessalonians 2:1 For yourselves, brethren, know our entrance in unto you, that it was not in vain: **2:2** But even after that we had suffered before, and were shamefully entreated, as ye know, at Philippi, we were bold in our God to speak unto you the gospel [the whole Word of God] of God with much contention.

The faithful recognize the words of truth by the inspiration of God's Spirit, because of their zeal for God and their love to live by every Word of God. They love God and by God's Spirit and a diligent study of the Word of God they recognize the truth of God.

Paul then goes on to tell them of his honesty in his preaching, and his deep love for God and for them.

2:3 For our exhortation was not of deceit, nor of uncleanness, nor in guile: **2:4** But as we were allowed of God to be put in trust with the gospel, even so we speak; not as pleasing men, but [to please God] God, which trieth [tests us] our hearts.

Paul did not seek advantage over them, neither wealth nor adulation; he did not seek for anyone to follow him, but for all to follow God. How unlike many of the leaders and elders of today's spiritual Ekklesia.

2:5 For neither at any time used we flattering words, as ye know, nor a cloke of covetousness; God is witness: **2:6** Nor of men sought we glory, neither of you, nor yet of others, when we might have been burdensome, as the apostles of Christ.

Paul cherished the brethren with all his heart as did Jesus Christ; who lived and died to reconcile mankind with God the Father.

2:7 But we were gentle among you, even as a nurse cherisheth her children: **2:8** So being affectionately desirous of you, we were willing to have imparted unto you, not the gospel of God only, but also our own souls, because ye were dear unto us. **2:9** For ye remember, brethren, our labour and travail: for labouring night and day, because we would not be chargeable unto any of you, we preached unto you the gospel of God. **2:10** Ye are witnesses, and God also, how holily and justly and unblameably we behaved ourselves among you that believe:

2:11 As ye know how we exhorted and comforted and charged [taught] every one of you, [cherishing you] as a father doth his children, **2:12** That ye would walk worthy of God [by living as Christ lived, obeying God and doing those things which please God], who hath called you unto his kingdom and glory.

The pillars who receive and live by every Word of God with great joy will be filled with the works of faith; which is the effectual working of the Word of God in us.

2:13 For this cause also thank we God without ceasing, because, when ye received the word of God which ye heard of us, ye received it not as the word of men, **but as it is in truth, the word of God, which effectually worketh also in you that believe.**

The Thessalonians and today's pillars experience many trials

2:14 For ye, brethren, became followers [God's faithful are fellow brethren with others who have suffered for the faith.] of the churches of God which in Judaea are in Christ Jesus: for **ye also have suffered like things of your own countrymen, even as they have of the Jews: 2:15** Who both killed the Lord Jesus, and their own prophets, and have persecuted us; and they please not God, and are contrary to all men: **2:16** Forbidding us to speak to the Gentiles that they might be saved, to fill up their sins alway: for the wrath is come upon them to the uttermost.

My friends, if these people suffered for the truth of God in the Mosaic Assembly of that day; do not think it strange if today's pillars who love to live by every Word of God, are also persecuted and chastised by their brethren in today's corporate assemblies.

Remember that they rejected any zeal for God's Word before they rejected us. Be strong in the Spirit and faint not, for the day will soon come when those who rejected a love for godliness will return to their first loving zeal to learn and live by God's Word, with sincere repentance and rejoicing in God's deliverance.

Paul mentions that he would like to visit them but was delayed

2:17 But we, brethren, being taken from you for a short time in presence, not in heart, endeavoured the more abundantly to see your face with great desire. **2:18** Wherefore we would have come unto you, even I Paul, once and again; but Satan hindered us.

The desire of Paul's heart is that all of the pillars remain faithful to love God and to live by every Word of God, and so be among the chosen at the resurrection to spirit and the coming of Christ.

Brethren that is my hope also; that all the called to God through Christ, should overcome and be chosen as a part of the bride!

2:19 For what is our hope, or joy, or crown of rejoicing? Are not even **ye in the presence of our Lord Jesus Christ at his coming? 2:20 For ye are our glory and joy.**

1 Thessalonians 3

Paul reveals that he is at Athens and is sending this letter by Timothy for the purpose of confirming and establishing the pillars of faith at Thessaloniki.

1 Thessalonians 3:1 Wherefore when we could no longer forbear, we thought it good to be left at Athens alone; **3:2** And sent Timotheus, our brother, and minister of God, and our fellowlabourer in the gospel of Christ, **to establish you, and to comfort you concerning your faith: 3:3** That no man should be moved by these afflictions: for yourselves know that we are appointed thereunto.

Paul, suffering persecution and opposition himself, was deeply concerned that the pillars in Thessaloniki should not waver during persecution.

Today, as the scriptures have warned us (Mat 24:5, 24:11, Jude), the spiritual Ekklesia is filled with deceivers who try to lead the brethren away from any zeal to live by every Word of God to follow idols of men and false traditions, and to persecute the faithful pillars that they cannot deceive.

3:4 For verily, when we were with you, we told you before that we should suffer tribulation; even as it came to pass, and ye know. **3:5** For this cause, when I could no longer forbear, **I sent to know your faith, lest by some means the tempter have tempted you, and our labour be in vain.**

Paul rejoiced at the steadfastness of the brethren at Thessaloniki when he received Timothy's report.

Today God has not left his pillars without support and encouragement for their zeal!

3:6 But now when Timotheus came from you unto us, and brought us good tidings of your faith and charity [true godly love, which is living by every Word of God], and that ye have good remembrance of us always, desiring greatly to see us, as we also to see you: **3:7** Therefore, brethren, we were comforted over you in all our affliction and distress by your faith: **3:8** For now we live [rejoice], if ye stand fast in the Lord.

Paul prays for the zealous of Thessaloniki and desires to meet with those pillars, being full of great joy over their steadfastness.

The pillars of today who are greatly scattered, also pray for one another in deep concern over all the deception and persecution that each must bear, praying to confirm their strength of zeal to stand on the solid foundation of the whole Word of God; and we long for the day that we will meet with one another and be with our LORD!

3:9 For what thanks can we render to God again for you, for all the joy wherewith we joy for your sakes before our God; **3:10** Night and day praying exceedingly that we might see your face, and might perfect that which is lacking in your faith? **3:11** Now God himself and our Father, and our Lord Jesus Christ, direct our way unto you.

Paul prays that he might see his friends and that they will be perfected in their faith and love of God.

If we have faith in God: We will have the works of faith and we will live by every Word of God! We are to abound in love of God to do God's will, and our love for God will result in also loving people.

Proper godly love of people is built on the foundation of love for God and the keeping of the whole Word of God, which teaches us how to love God and humanity.

3:12 And the Lord make you to increase and abound in love one toward another, and toward all men, even as we do toward you: **3:13 To the end he may stablish your hearts unblameable in holiness before God, even our Father, at the coming of our Lord Jesus Christ with all his saints.**

Being unblameable in holiness before God the Father; means to be in FULL COMPLETE UNITY with God Almighty! In thoughts and in deeds!

We achieve that FULL UNITY with God by following the Lamb whithersoever he goeth (Rev 14:4), by following the lead of God's Spirit into all TRUTH and by an uncompromising obedience to all of God's Word and Will; thereby internalizing the very mind and nature of God!

Paul encourages the faithful to grow more and more in sanctification [set apartness to God and separated from worldliness] and their zeal to please God.

1 Thessalonians 4

The pillars are taught and encouraged by Paul to live according to the scriptures.

Those who are pillars today must also live by every Word of God the Father, growing continually in godliness; which is well pleasing to God (Mat 4:4)

1 Thessalonians 4:1 Furthermore then we beseech you, brethren, and exhort you by the Lord Jesus, that **as ye have received of us how ye ought to walk and to please God, so ye would abound more and more. 4:2** For ye know what commandments we gave you by the Lord Jesus. **4:3** For this is the will of God, even your sanctification, that ye should abstain from fornication [pornea; all sexual sin and its spiritual corollary which is disloyalty to God and idolatry]:

We are to flee from all sexual sins and disloyalty, and to be absolutely faithful to our spouses [a man and a woman joined together by God]; which was instituted to teach us the virtue of deep abiding love and LOYALTY to our espoused eternal Husband Jesus Christ.

4:4 That every one of you should know how to possess his vessel in sanctification and honour; **4:5** Not in the lust of concupiscence [evil thoughts, plans and imaginations including vicariously sinning by delighting in watching others sin], even as the Gentiles [as those who do not know God] which know not God: **4:6** That no man go beyond and **defraud his brother in any matter** [Including deceiving many away from any zeal for God and thereby defrauding people of their salvation and their crowns. God will correct the deceivers who now walk respected and unafraid among the assemblies.]: because that the Lord is the avenger of all such, as we also have forewarned you and testified.

We were not called to remain in the uncleanness of sin: We were called to come out of [and to cast away] all sin. To become clean, pure and holy, just as God the Father is holy.

4:7 For God hath not called us unto uncleanness, but unto holiness.

Today, many brethren are like those looking into a large mirror who close their eyes to their blemishes and imperfections and proclaim ourselves clean of sin and godly, when we are not clean at all.

Our many compromises which we see as only little things are all seen by God, and are big things to him. They prevent us from being like him who has no sin, and they are a blot on our Feasts, being unacceptable blemishes that the Bridegroom will not tolerate (2 Peter 2:13). Either we cleanse ourselves or we will be rejected by God the Father as a part of the collective bride for his Son.

4:8 He therefore that despiseth [Those who despise others who are zealous to live by every Word of God; despise the author of God's Word, God Almighty.], despiseth not man, but God, who hath also given unto us his holy Spirit.

Do not despise zeal to live by every Word of, and by the Will of God. Let us all work diligently to internalize the very nature of our beloved Father and our espoused Husband through living by their every Word!

If we love God and are enthusiastic to do God's will, then we will also love mankind just as Jesus Christ loved humanity and gave his life to ransom man from sincerely repented PAST sin.

4:9 But as touching brotherly love ye need not that I write unto you: for ye yourselves are taught of God to love one another.

Be honest and work hard, not being lazy; both in learning [study and thinking] and applying the things of God in our daily lives.

4:10 And indeed ye do it toward all the brethren which are in all Macedonia: but we beseech you, brethren, that ye increase more and more;
4:11 And that ye study to be quiet, and to do your own business, and to

work with your own hands, as we commanded you; **4:12** That ye may walk honestly toward them that are without, and that ye may have lack of nothing.

Study hard and be honest and careful to live a Christ-like life.

Now come words of encouragement concerning the dead in Christ, and the reward of those found faithful at his coming.

4:13 But I would not have you to be ignorant, brethren, concerning them which are asleep, that ye sorrow not, even as others which have no hope. **4:14 For if we believe that Jesus died and rose again, even so them also which sleep in Jesus will God bring with him.**

God the Father will raise up the faithful just as he raised up Jesus Christ, and Christ will come with them to rule the earth.

Just as God raised up the sinless Christ; he will also raise up those who allow Christ to live in them and who are filled with Christ-like zeal to live by every Word of God (Psalm 69:9).

4:15 For this we say unto you by the word of the Lord, that we which are alive and remain unto the coming of the Lord shall not prevent [precede] them which are asleep.

The dead who were faithful and zealous through Jesus Christ living in them, will awaken and rise up to God in heaven (Rev 15, 19); they shall be changed to spirit and rise with the dead into heaven for the Wedding Feast of the Lamb (Eph 2:6). After which they shall return to rule the earth with Messiah the Christ their collective Husband (Rev 15, 19)!

4:16 For the Lord himself shall descend from heaven with a shout, with the voice of the archangel, and with the trump of God: and the dead in Christ shall rise first:

> **Revelation 10:7** But in the days of the voice of the seventh angel, when he shall begin to sound, the mystery of God should be finished, as he hath declared to his servants the prophets.

If we sincerely repent of breaking God's law and then STOP sinning and continue in living by every Word of God, we shall be raised up to eternal life.

> **1 Corinthians 15:50** Now this I say, brethren, that flesh and blood cannot inherit the kingdom of God; neither doth corruption inherit incorruption.

If we remain carnal and not subject to the Word of God; we shall NOT enter the resurrection to spirit.

15:51 Behold, I shew you a mystery; We shall not all sleep, but we shall all be changed**, 15:52** In a moment, in the twinkling of an eye, at the last trump: for the trumpet shall sound, and the dead shall be raised incorruptible, and we shall be changed. **15:53** For this corruptible must put on incorruption, and this mortal must put on immortality.

15:54 So when this corruptible shall have put on incorruption, [the physical bodies of the faithful will be changed to spirit] and this mortal shall have put on immortality, then shall be brought to pass the saying that is written, Death is swallowed up in victory.

15:55 O death, where is thy sting? O grave, where is thy victory? **15:56** The sting of death is sin; and the strength of sin is the [Sin is the breaking of the law for which the penalty is death.] law.

15:57 But thanks be to God, which giveth us the victory [over commandment and law breaking, which is sin] through our Lord Jesus Christ.

15:58 Therefore, my beloved brethren, be ye stedfast, unmovable, always abounding in the work of the Lord, forasmuch as ye know that your labour is not in vain in the Lord.

Take a stand to keep the Word of God without compromise; and we shall, by internalizing the very nature of God as defined by his Word be changed into spirit just as God is spirit!

1 Thessalonians 4:17 Then we which are alive and remain shall be caught up together with them in the clouds, to meet the Lord in the air: and so shall we ever be with the Lord.

4:18 Wherefore comfort one another with these words.

1 Thessalonians 5

Paul begins to instruct the pillars of our day about the onset of the tribulation, first teaching that the vast majority will be taken completely by surprise.

1 Thessalonians 5:1 But of the times and the seasons, brethren, ye have no need that I write unto you. **5:2** For yourselves know perfectly that the day of the Lord so cometh as a thief in the night.

Paul was indeed writing to those people at that time however I would point out that all scripture was written and preserved for all of God's people including us today. Whether Paul and the other writers knew about us is not important, the fact is that God knew the plan and had these scriptures preserved for us

The great tribulation at the end of this age of sin will come as a great surprise to the vast majority of humanity, including the vast majority of the Ekklesia who are lax and lukewarm, rejecting the warnings and the biblical signs in favor of their false traditions.

The scriptures say that it is during a time of peace that these things will come suddenly [unexpectedly]:

Daniel 8:25 And through his policy also he shall cause craft to prosper in his hand [the king of the North will make the New Europe prosperous]; and he shall magnify himself in his heart, **and by peace shall destroy many**: he shall also stand up against the Prince of princes; but he shall be broken without hand.

1 Thessalonians 5:3 For when they shall say, Peace and safety; then sudden [Strong's G1601 completely unexpected, sudden, unforeseen, by surprise] destruction cometh upon them [Jerusalem, Judea and greater Israel], as travail upon a woman with child; and they shall not escape.

After the coming bloody peace will seem to be achieved, and when that peace is declared as the man of sin goes to the Holy Place; sudden and immediate destruction will come upon Jerusalem and Judah.

God Almighty will bring all the Islamic countries except Egypt [the nations of Psalm 83] against Judah and Jerusalem, and Europe will intervene to stop the slaughter: Then the main nations of greater Israel will quickly fall into economic collapse and many troubles as well.

The children of light are pillars who stand unalterably on every Word of God like the Thessalonians did, they are zealous and faithful to God and to every Word of God.

Having been warned and being the children of LIGHT through their zeal to live by every Word of God, the spiritual pillars will see and understand the signs and will NOT be taken by surprise.

The sinners of the world's nations and the spiritually lukewarm and spiritually blind children of darkness, including many in today's spiritual Ekklesia; will reject the scriptures and insist that Jesus was wrong in Matthew 24:15; and that there must still be 3 1/2 years before the tribulation, or that some physical temple or renewed daily sacrifice must first come, and so will be deceived by their own false traditions and beliefs.

First the abomination, the man of sin will be set up in the Vatican and then within about 75 days he will go to the holy place. Then the world's peoples and the worldly spiritual lax brethren will not believe the warnings and will be caught completely by surprise by the tribulation.

Only the pillars of today who are like the zealous of Thessaloniki will be alert and aware and will understand and will NOT be taken by surprise; they have been forewarned and when peace is about to be declared and the man of sin schedules his visit to the holy place the children of light will know that the tribulation is about to begin.

Jesus Christ himself said that when the abomination visits the holy place the tribulation will immediately begin.

The true Gospel being preached is NOT the sign of the beginning of any great tribulation; it is the sign of the actual coming of Christ to rule this earth.

> **Matthew 24:14** And this gospel of the kingdom shall be preached in all the world for a witness unto all nations; and **then shall the end come**.

The Gospel being preached is NOT the sign of the beginning of any great tribulation.

The preaching of the true Gospel will be continued by God's two prophets and by God's mighty angels; until the very coming of Jesus Christ with his saints!

This preaching will take place DURING the tribulation as well as before it, and is NOT a sign of the beginning of the tribulation: it is the sign of Christ's actual coming.

The sign of the beginning of the tribulation is the setting up of the final miracle working man of sin in the Vatican and his visit to the holy place about 75 days later.

> **24:15** When ye therefore shall see the abomination of desolation, spoken of by Daniel the prophet, **stand in the holy place,** (whoso readeth, let him understand:)

This abomination is set up as a miracle working pope in Rome and then goes to the Holy Place [the whole Mount is Holy] within about 75 days, triggering the tribulation.

When the abomination [the final false prophet] is set up in Rome, he has only a total of 1,335 days before he is destroyed (Dan 12, Rev 19:20).

1,335 minus 1,260 for the tribulation, begins the tribulation about 75 days after the final miracle working abomination is set up in the papacy in Rome.

When you see the miracle working abomination set up in Rome, and call for a New Europe; then know that the tribulation is imminent and will begin when he goes to the Mount.

When we understand that some will leave the land to run to safety and some will not, it should be self-evident that a split between the zealous for godliness and the lukewarm [being devoid of any zeal for the practical application of the Word of God] of Revelation 3:14-22; is inevitable.

It should also be self-evident from the obvious apostasy in the Ekklesia today; that the prophesied falling away of many from any zeal for God, has and is taking place.

The spiritually wise will know that the tribulation will begin within 75 days, when they see this abomination set up in Rome. After that God will send his Two Servants who will take the zealous to God's refuge as one of their first acts. That does not mean that those two will actually go there, it means that their miraculous intervention will allow the faithful brethren to go to the place which God has prepared for those that love him.

The spiritually slothful in today's Spiritual Ekklesia will not understand until the tribulation begins with the occupation of Jerusalem.

Then many of them will see their error and sincerely repent, only to be forced to prove the sincerity of their repentance by persevering in great tribulation. The great tribulation will begin when the miracle working false prophet visits the holy place within about 75 days after being set up as pope in the Vatican.

> **24:16** Then let them which be in Judaea flee into the mountains: **24:17** Let him which is on the housetop not come down to take any thing out of his house: **24:18** Neither let him which is in the field return back to take his clothes. **24:19** And woe unto them that are with child, and to them that give suck in those days! **24:20** But pray ye that your flight be not in the winter, neither on the sabbath day: **24:21** For then shall be great tribulation, such as was not since the beginning of the world to this time, no, nor ever shall be.

It is when this final false prophet is set up in Rome and then goes to the Holy Place within about 75 days; that the great tribulation will begin: Immediately, at that time, so quickly that one should not even go home to fetch his coat! This we have on the direct authority of Jesus Christ.

This statement is repeated in a slightly different context by the apostle Paul.

> **1 Thessalonians 5:3** For 1063 when 3752 they shall say 3004 5725, Peace 1515 and 2532 safety 803; then 5119 sudden160 [unexpected,

surprise] destruction 3639 cometh upon 2186 5731 them 846, as 5618 travail 5604 upon 1722a woman with child 1064 2192 5723; and 2532 they shall 1628 0 not 3364 escape 1628 5632.

When we add Christ's words to Paul's we can see that the proclamation that peace has been achieved and the abomination going to the Holy Place; both happen at about the same time.

1 Thessalonians 5:4 But ye, brethren, **are not in darkness, that that day should overtake you as a thief.**

The beginning of the great tribulation and the time of the coming of Christ will not be concealed from God's faithful zealous pillars. They WILL KNOW, because they are the wise in Christ; for they have been warned and they have BELIEVED the warnings and they are faithful and zealous to live by every Word of our God!

Daniel 12:10 Many shall be purified, and made white, and tried; but the wicked shall do wickedly: and none of the wicked shall understand; **but the wise** [zealous to learn and to keep the whole Word of God] **shall understand.**

1 Thessalonians 5:5 Ye [pillars who stand on the firm foundation of the whole Word of God] **are all the children of light, and the children of the day: we are not of the night, nor of darkness.**

Those who love God enough to be zealous to learn and to keep his Word are instructed to be soberly watchful for the signs, and to be prepared so that they will not be taken by surprise by these things.

5:6 Therefore **let us not sleep, as do others; but let us watch and be sober.**

Let us awaken and turn to a passionate zeal to live by every Word of God and watch soberly and intently for the signs which God has given to us so that we may know when these things will be fulfilled.

5:7 For they [the Laodiceans of today are drunk with pride and are spiritually asleep] that sleep sleep in the night; and they that be drunken are drunken in the night.

Those who are drunk with pride and conceit, and who say that there must be 3 1/2 years after a declaration of peace, in direct contradiction to Jesus Christ in Matthew 24:15 and the apostle Paul in 1 Thessalonians 5:3; will be taken by surprise for they think they know everything and really know nothing, being spiritually blind and wretched and naked, not being zealous for the Word of God and relying on their own imaginations.

Laodicea [Meaning: The People Will be Judged]

> To Laodicea Jesus identifies himself as the faithful and true witness of what they are truly like. They think themselves spiritually rich and have no idea what Jesus Christ really thinks of them. Jesus here tells them their problems straight out, but they are proud and wilfully blind to reality.

> Emphasizing that his message to Laodicea is true and coming from Christ's faithful love for them as a warning in the hope that they might repent and be saved. Jesus also calls himself the "beginning of the creation of God;" clearly meaning that Christ is the Creator who began the creation of all things.

> **Revelation 3:14** And unto the angel of the church of the Laodiceans write; These things saith the Amen, the faithful and true witness, the beginning of the creation of God;

> Laodicea is spiritually lukewarm, professing godliness while keeping the commandments according to their own imaginations instead of keeping them the way that God commands.

> They pay lip service to godliness without any zeal to learn and live by every Word of God. Their zeal is for their own ways and what they think, and for their own false traditions and their idols of men and not for what God says. They stand on false traditions and proudly think they know it all; refusing any spiritual growth they are stagnant or even falling backward in their spiritual condition.

> They are hot for their own traditions, and for the teachings of their idols of men, and cold for zealously keeping the whole Word of God as God has commanded them. This mixture of hot for their idols of men and corporate entities, and a lack of zeal to keep the Word of God makes them lukewarm and revolting to God teh father and Jesus Christ.

> They are idolaters of men and the traditions of men; proud, thinking that they know it all spiritually and therefore they refuse correction from God or man and they reject the Word of God for their own ways, rejecting any growth in truth and refusing to turn from error, they fall deeper and deeper into error and sin.

Because these folks have rejected living by every Word of God and following Christ above our idols of men, they will be rejected by Jesus Christ into the correction of great tribulation, in the hope that through the correction of the flesh the spirit may be saved.

3:15 I know thy works, that thou art neither cold nor hot: I would thou wert cold or hot. **3:16** So then because thou art lukewarm, and neither cold nor hot, **I will spue thee out of my mouth** [they will be rejected by Christ into severe correction].

Proud and self-willed, they think they are spiritually rich and know it all, having need of no spiritual growth, and reject the promised increase in spiritual knowledge and understanding promised for the last days (Dan 12).

They reject any part of scripture that they do not want to follow, saying it is for others; or that it is not reliable; and are so proud that they have no idea how spiritually wretched, miserable and naked of godly righteousness they really are.

They are wilfully blind to their own condition and to the things of God that disprove their own false ways; They lack the garments of righteousness and are naked before God, their many sins exposed to Him; beginning with the sins of pride, stubborn self will, self justification and self approval.

3:17 Because thou sayest, I am rich [spiritually], and increased with goods [spiritual knowledge], and have need of nothing [no one not even Jesus Christ (the Word of God) can tell them anything]; and knowest not that thou art [spiritually] wretched, and miserable, and [spiritually] poor [knowing almost nothing of God as they ought to know it], and blind [wilfully blind to their wretched spiritual state], and naked [naked of any true godly righteousness, not being zealous to keep the Word of God]:

Christ counsels those with the Laodicean attitude to buy spiritual gold in the fire of tribulation; that they may become spiritually rich.

They are bidden to sincerely repent of their prideful sins so that the nakedness of their wickedness may be covered by the application of the sacrifice of Christ; so that they may receive God's Holy Spirit and the white raiment of the righteousness of the zealous keeping of the whole Word of God.

They are commanded to anoint their eyes and open them to see themselves as God sees them, and to sincerely repent from their pride and false ways and to turn away from their idols of men and false traditions to follow the Spirit of God into all truth; rejecting all error and sin to embrace godly truth that they might be saved.

3:18 I counsel thee to buy of me [spiritual] gold tried in the fire [during the period of correction in the fire of tribulation], that thou mayest be [become spiritually rich] rich; and white raiment [the righteousness of zealously keeping the whole Word of God], that thou mayest be clothed, and that the shame of thy nakedness [that our sins might be covered by the righteousness of God] do not appear; and anoint thine eyes with eyesalve, that thou mayest see [open our eyes to see ourselves as God sees us, to see ourselves as we really are so that we can repent and be saved].

Jesus reminds these folks that he rebukes them only because he truly loves them and is not willing that they should perish. They are rejected only because they first rejected God the Father and Jesus Christ, refusing to follow Christ and refusing to live by every Word of God in Christ-like zeal.

Jesus Christ tells those with this Laodicean attitude, which is the overwhelming attitude in the Ekklesia today; to REPENT of their pride and self-righteousness. and to REPENT of trusting in their idols of men and false traditions.

Jesus Christ tells us to turn to him and turn to a zeal for the whole Word of God, to learn it and to keep it; to turn from our false idols and false traditions and to become zealous to remove error and embrace the truth of God!

3:19 As many as I love, I rebuke and chasten: be zealous therefore, and repent.

Jesus is warning and calling each one of his straying sheep; He wants them to open up to him, to reject idols and to follow him, to be zealous to remove sin and embrace God's righteous truth, to internalize the solid meat of the Word of God in fellowship with Christ.

They have an open invitation from Jesus Christ who is gladly willing to accept them, if they would only open up their eyes and turn to Him!

3:20 Behold, I stand at the door, and knock: if any man hear my voice, and open the door, I will come in to him, and will sup [eat; internalize the Word of God] with him, and he with me.

Those who justify themselves face severe correction in the tribulation and only those who overcome this Laodicean attitude of pride and self-centeredness will be resurrected to spirit. Those who sincerely repent of the sins of Laodicea will be in the resurrection to eternal life and will have a place in the eternal government of God.

3:21 To him that overcometh will I grant to sit with me in my throne, even as I also overcame, and am set down with my Father in his throne.

3:22 He that hath an ear, let him hear what the Spirit saith unto the churches.

As the seventh and last assembly, Laodicea has all of the problems of all the other churches.

That is because pride is the chief cause of most of the various problems. Today both mainstream professing Christianity and the Brotherhood are full of pride and idolatry, rejecting any biblical thing they do not agree with, as unreliable or applying only to others.

They think of themselves as the repository of all wisdom and truth, and refuse any zeal to keep the whole Word of God, in order to follow their corporate idols, idols of men and there own false traditions.

The pillars of God who stand on the whole Word of God, are to believe and trust in the Word of God and must never trust in idols of men and the false traditions of men.

1 Thessalonians 5:8 But let us, who are of the day, be sober, putting on the breastplate of faith and love; and for an helmet, the hope of salvation. 5:9 For God hath not appointed us [the faithful pillars are not appointed to such correction] **to wrath,** but to obtain salvation by our Lord Jesus Christ, **5:10** Who died for us, that, whether we wake or sleep, we should live together with him.

The diligent for God and the whole Word of God, should comfort one another with these things.

5:11 Wherefore comfort yourselves together, and edify one another, even as also ye do.

Brethren, we know that the violence of today and the coming wars will reset world conditions so that a genuine peace can be made. We know this because the Word of God tells us that "Peace and Safety" will be declared before the tribulation comes! There will be an end to these wars which will bring a genuine peace deal; we have the Word of God telling us so!

As you see these things being fulfilled; as you see these wars come and go and a genuine dialogue for peace take place; as you see a peace deal ratified; as you see the miracle working abomination the man of sin, being set up in the Vatican and bringing a New Europe to life: You can know that the great tribulation WILL begin when he goes to the Holy Place, for it is the very Word of Jesus Christ himself!

We are NOT to esteem any person who teaches others to reject any zeal to learn and to keep the whole Word of God. We are to reject all those who teach us to make idols of men and false traditions and who compromise with God's Word. They are the children of darkness, refusing the light of God for their own folly.

Those faithful to God and his commandments should look about and mark out those who labor to turn the brethren to God, and who admonish all the brethren to turn with zeal to their God as true godly people!

5:12 And we beseech you, brethren, to know them which labour among you, and are over you in the Lord, and admonish you; **5:13** And to esteem them very highly in love for their work's sake. And be at peace among yourselves.

5:14 Now we exhort you, brethren, warn them that are unruly [contentious against sound doctrine and godly conduct], comfort the feebleminded [the weak in understanding], support the [spiritually weak by teaching them sound doctrine] weak, be patient toward all men.

When we are abused or rejected, always follow godliness and do not give place to anger, but do good by teaching and living godliness.

5:15 See that none render evil for evil unto any man; but ever follow that which is good, both among yourselves, and to all men. **5:16** Rejoice evermore.

Rejoice in your calling and pray without ceasing for God's help through his Spirit, so that we may endure to the very end and overcome all things.

Rejoice in our trials knowing that the Master Potter is molding us into a precious eternal vessel according to his will!

5:17 Pray without ceasing. **5:18** In every thing give thanks: for this is the will of God in Christ Jesus concerning you.

Be grateful to God for our calling and his many blessings and promises; which are sure and will be fulfilled for us if we faint not. Do not quench the Spirit by compromising with God's Word.

5:19 Quench not the Spirit.

5:20 Despise not prophesyings.

Do not despise the promised advances in knowledge and understanding (Dan 12). God reveals his will to those who are diligent to live by his Word when the time is at hand.

Let us embrace the truth, discarding error, growing in knowledge and progressing in understanding. Enthusiastically live by every Word of God and watch diligently as these things unfold and remember the signs and warnings that God has given to those who love him and do that which is pleasing in his sight.

5:21 Prove all things; hold fast that which is good.

Prove all things by the Word of God!

Utterly reject any compromise with God's Word and reject all toleration of sin in the same manner that God our Father in heaven utterly rejects any spiritual uncleanness in his temple [his people]! Avoid even the mere appearance of evil so that the light of your example may shine brightly

5:22 Abstain from all appearance of evil.

5:23 And the very God of peace sanctify [set us apart from all worldliness and sin] you wholly; and I pray God **your whole spirit and soul and body be preserved blameless** [without any willful sin] unto the coming of our Lord Jesus Christ.

Become blameless as touching the Word of God, and fully internalize the mind and nature of God the Father and the Son, so that you will come into a complete unity of mind, spirit, attitude and deeds with Almighty God!

5:24 Faithful is he that calleth you, who also will do it.

5:25 Brethren, pray for us. **5:26** Greet all the brethren with an holy kiss.

5:27 I charge you by the Lord that this epistle be read unto all the holy brethren.

5:28 The grace of our Lord Jesus Christ be with you. Amen.

Dear brethren: pray for me also, that I may exhort according to God's will. Pray for all the brethren; that they may all endure and overcome being filled with the gift of God's Spirit, and full of a tremendous zeal for our great God and his wondrous ways.

May the light of God and his ways shine brightly through his people!

Second Thessalonians

2 Thessalonians 1

2 Thessalonians 1:1 Paul, and Silvanus, and Timotheus, unto the church of the Thessalonians in God our Father and the Lord Jesus Christ: **1:2** Grace unto you, and peace, from God our Father and the Lord Jesus Christ.

Paul thanks God for the faith and strong spiritual growth of the pillars of Thessaloniki. The pillars in the church today are also patiently enduring persecution from without and even from within the Ekklesia for their diligence and zeal to stand on and grow in the whole Word of God.

1:3 We are bound to thank God always for you, brethren, as it is meet, because that your faith groweth exceedingly, and the charity of every one of you all toward each other aboundeth; **1:4** So that we ourselves glory in you in the churches of God for your patience and faith in all your persecutions and tribulations that ye endure:

Paul and the brotherhood are much impressed and encouraged by the steadfastness, spiritual growth and diligence of the pillars of Thessaloniki to learn and to keep God's Word, and by their faithful endurance. Let us persevere in these same things today so that we may also be accounted pillars of the faith, standing unmovable on the strong foundation of the whole Word of God.

Ephesians 2:20 And **are built upon the foundation of the apostles and prophets** [the Holy Scriptures written by the prophets and apostles], **Jesus Christ himself being the chief corner stone**; **2:21** In whom all the building fitly framed together groweth unto an holy temple in the Lord: **2:22** In whom ye also are builded together for an habitation of God through the Spirit.

The pillars who stand unmovable on the whole Word of God will be spared the tribulation [Revelation 3 Philadelphia message] and inherit the Kingdom of God, while those who persecute them will be corrected in great tribulation.

2 Thessalonians 1:5 Which is a manifest token of the righteous judgment of God, that ye may be counted worthy of the kingdom of God, for which ye also suffer: **1:6** Seeing it is a righteous thing with God **to recompense tribulation to them that trouble you;**

God is righteous to spare those who suffer for their faith and for their obedience to him, and he will correct those who persecute the faithful saints for their zeal for God. During which correction many of Laodicea will sincerely repent and when Christ comes they will be accepted by him.

The sincerely repentant will rejoice at the deliverance of Christ when he comes and destroys the armies of wickedness and removes Satan and his demons from having any power or influence to deceive the nations.

1:7 And to you who are troubled rest [endure patiently until the day of resurrection] with us, when the Lord Jesus shall be revealed from heaven with his mighty angels, **1:8** In flaming fire taking vengeance on them that know not God, and that obey not the gospel of our Lord Jesus Christ:

Many of the elect will rest in the grave like Paul does, until Jesus Christ comes with his angels to gather them up.

1:9 Who shall be punished with everlasting destruction from the presence of the Lord [speaking of those who in the end utterly refuse to repent], and from the glory of his power; **1:10** When he shall come to be glorified in his saints, and to be admired in all them that believe (because our testimony among you was believed) in that day.

The resurrected saints will glorify their Husband at the wedding feast in heaven, and they shall be glorified with him in their complete unity of Spirit with God the Father and with Jesus Christ.

1:11 Wherefore also we pray always for you, that our God would count you worthy of this calling [We can be accounted worthy because of our Christ-like zeal to live by every Word of God.], and fulfil all the good pleasure [fulfill all of God's will] of his goodness, and the work of faith with power [doing the powerful works of faith in keeping God's Word and overcoming all deception and persecution]: **1:12** That the name of our Lord Jesus Christ may be glorified in you, and ye in him [so that the faithful called out may be in complete unity with God the Father and Jesus Christ], according to the grace of our God and the Lord Jesus Christ.

2 Thessalonians 2

2 Thessalonians 2:1 Now we beseech you, brethren, by the coming of our Lord Jesus Christ, and by our gathering together unto him, **2:2** That ye be not soon shaken in mind, or be troubled, neither by spirit, nor by word, nor by letter as from us, as that the day of Christ is at hand.

Do not allow men who would use the threat of the tribulation and Christ's coming to deceive you into following them instead of standing on the biblical signs and the Word of God.

First, there will be a general falling away from any zeal to learn and to live by every Word of God. People cannot fall away from something they were never a part of, this refers directly to today's spiritual called out Ekklesia. This great falling away has been happening for decades now and is near a climax and today's Ekklesia has turned away from God to follow idols of men and corporate entities.

2:3 Let no man deceive you by any means: for that day shall not come, except there come a falling away first, . . .

This refers to the general falling away from zeal to live by every Word of God, warned of by Jesus, Jude, Paul and others.

> **Jude 1:3** Beloved, when I gave all diligence to write unto you of the common salvation, it was needful for me to write unto you, and exhort you that **ye should earnestly contend for the faith which was once delivered unto the saints.**
>
> **1:4** For there are certain men crept in unawares, who were before of old ordained to this condemnation, ungodly men, turning the grace of our God into lasciviousness, and denying the only Lord God, and our Lord Jesus Christ [denying their authority through refusing to live by every Word of God].

This is what has happened in today's spiritual Ekklesia over the past decades and it is what this blog is reminding the brethren about. Almighty God said this present general apostasy from sound doctrine would come in these last days and this has been fulfilled before our very eyes.

We have apostatized from any zeal for the practical application of God's Word into a lax, lukewarm, careless attitude towards doing what God has commanded; and instead we do what we think is right and exalt our leaders and organizations as our idols above the Word of God.

2 Thessalonians 2:3. . . . and that man of sin be revealed, the son of perdition; **2:4** Who opposeth and exalteth himself above all that is called God, or that is worshipped; so that he as God sitteth in the temple of God, shewing himself that he is God.

This "man of sin" the "son of perdition" [son of damnation] is an abominable person to God and is the abomination spoken of by Jesus Christ (Mat 24:15) and Daniel (Dan 12).

He presents himself [claims to be man's ultimate moral authority] as God sitting in the Temple of God as he sits on his throne in the Vatican.

He will be set up doing miracles in the Vatican, and sitting on his throne in the Vatican he will take the place of all that is called god, presenting himself as the world's ultimate moral authority; and he will appear to be like God sitting in the false "Temple of God" [the Vatican] in place of God.

He will deceive the whole world except for the very elect and to the whole world he will appear to be in place of God with all the authority and prerogatives of God in the supposed absence of God.

He claims to be sitting in the temple of God as he sits on his throne in the Vatican. For he will set himself up as mankind's ultimate moral authority in place of God; just as the popes have claimed for generations, by claiming to be representative of and acting for God while God is far off somewhere.

The Popes are seen as acting in place of God until Christ returns, and therefore acting with the full authority of God; being God, in place of God, in the supposed absence of God.

1. "Those whom the Pope of Rome doth separate, it is not a man that separates them but God. For the Pope holdeth place on earth, not simply of a man but of the true God....dissolves, not by human but rather by divine authority....I am in all and above all, so that God Himself and I, the vicar of God, hath both one consistory, and I am able to do almost all that God can do...wherefore, if those things that I do be said not to be done of man, but of God, what do you make of me but God? Again, if prelates of the Church be called of Constantine for gods, I then being above all prelates, seem by this reason to be above all gods." Decretales Domini Gregori ix Translatione Episcoporum, (on the Transference of Bishops), title 7, chapter 3; Corpus Juris Canonice (2nd Leipzig ed., 1881), col. 99; (Paris, 1612), tom. 2, Decretales, col. 205 (while Innocent III was Pope).

2. "The Pope is of great authority and power, that he is able to modify, declare, or interpret even divine laws. The Pope can modify divine law, since his power is not of man, but of God, and he acts as vicegerent of God upon earth..." Lucius Ferraris, in "Prompta Bibliotheca Canonica, Juridica, Moralis, Theologica, Ascetica, Polemica, Rubristica, Historica", Volume V, article on "Papa, Article II", titled "Concerning the extent of Papal dignity, authority, or dominion and infallibility", #30, published in Petit-Montrouge (Paris) by J. P. Migne, 1858 edition.

3. "We confess that the Pope has power of changing Scripture and of adding to it, and taking from it, according to his will." Roman Catholic Confessions for Protestants Oath, Article XI, (Confessio Romano-Catholica in Hungaria Evangelicis publice praescripta te proposita, editi a Streitwolf), as recorded in Congressional Record of the U.S.A., House Bill 1523, Contested election case of Eugene C. Bonniwell, against Thos. S. Butler, Feb. 15, 1913.

4. **Every time a person calls the pope "Holy Father" they are calling him God!** The name "Holy Father" is found only **ONE** time in the **entire** Bible and it refers to God the Father! They are calling the pope by God's name! It is extreme blasphemy to call a man by God's name.

5. The papacy claims ALL the prerogatives of God, even if they are too smart to come out and publicly say they are God. And they allow themselves to be exalted as a god.

Falsely claiming that they have all the rights, prerogatives and moral authority of God on the earth and that they are the true church of God [today's corporate entities of the called out spiritual Ekklesia make the very same claims]; this final super abomination will sit in his temple in the Vatican, empowered by Satan with all deceitful signs, powers and wonders.

This is the abominable Nicolaitane church governance teaching also adopted by today's spiritual Ekklesia which places the leaders between the brethren and God and makes us anathema from God the Father and Jesus Christ.

2 Thessalonians 2:5 Remember ye not, that, when I was yet with you, I told you these things? **2:6** And now ye know what withholdeth [Jesus Christ is restraining the rise of this final man of sin until God's appointed time] that he might be revealed in his time.

2:7 For the mystery of iniquity doth already work: only he who now letteth [Jesus Christ the Restrainer will continue to restrain the rise of this wicked person until God's appointed time] will let [restrain], until he be taken out of the way.

It is Jesus Christ who holds back this ultimate great deception until the appointed time.

Because the elect who should be salting the earth with the salt and light of zealous godliness have in the majority lost their savor, Christ's intercession and restraint will be stopped and the man of sin will be set up in the Vatican. This is the stopping of the Daily intercession of the High Priest Jesus Christ for today's sinful Ekklesia before the throne of God in heaven.

Then when the son of perdition is set up in the Vatican doing great miracles to deceive the earth and calling for a New Federal Europe; our correction will begin within 75 days when this abomination goes to the Holy Place (Mat 24:15).

2:8 And then shall that Wicked be revealed, whom the Lord shall consume with the spirit of his mouth, and shall destroy with the brightness of his coming: **2:9** Even him, whose coming is after the working of Satan with all power and signs and lying wonders, **2:10** And with all deceivableness of unrighteousness in them that perish; because they received not the love of the truth, that they might be saved.

Those saints who have apostatized into lukewarmness from passionately living by every Word of God and now follow idols of men; will be corrected because they loved their pet ideas, corporate idols and false traditions more than they love the Word of God.

2:11 And for this cause God shall send them strong delusion, that they should believe a lie: **2:12** That they all might be damned who believed not the truth, but had pleasure in unrighteousness.

Paul then encourages the children of light, the pillars of God; who ARE zealous and love God and his Word above any man or personal pet idea or tradition.

2:13 But we are bound to give thanks alway to God for you, brethren beloved of the Lord, because God hath from the beginning chosen you to salvation through sanctification of the Spirit and belief of the truth: [being set apart by their love of and zeal for the truth of God]

2:14 Whereunto he called you by our gospel, to the obtaining of the glory of our Lord Jesus Christ.

2:15 Therefore, brethren, stand fast, and hold the traditions ["traditions" is a confusing word choice and is here referring to the doctrines of the Holy Scriptures which Paul has taught them, and not to the false traditions of men] which ye have been taught, whether by word, or our epistle.

Hold onto the tradition - the Doctrine of God's Word - of the truth, and reject all traditions of men which err from the scriptures.

2:16 Now our Lord Jesus Christ himself, and God, even our Father, which hath loved us, and hath given us everlasting consolation and good hope through grace, **2:17** Comfort your hearts, and stablish you in every good word and work.

May all the faithful called out be fully established in every Word of God, and in the Works of the Word of God!

2 Thessalonians 3

2 Thessalonians 3:1 Finally, brethren, pray for us, that the word of the Lord may have free course, and be glorified, even as it is with you: **3:2** And that we may be delivered from unreasonable and wicked men: for all men have not faith.

Please pray for me also, and for all the faithful pillars; and also pray that the faithless and lukewarm might awaken before they face a terrible correction.

3:3 But the Lord is faithful, who shall stablish you, and keep you from evil.

If we remain zealous and dedicated to our God, He will deliver us; for it is written that he will confirm his marriage covenant with and preserve his pillars according to his Word and Will; and that all the sincerely repentant who are zealous to learn and to live by every Word of God will rise up as a part of the collective spirit bride on that day!

3:4 And we have confidence in the Lord touching you, that ye both do and will do the things which we command you. **3:5** And the Lord direct your hearts into the love of God [which is the keeping of every Word of God], and into the patient waiting for Christ.

Today some brethren are wrongly taught to tolerate sin and doctrinal diversity in the name of organizational unity. Here is what the scriptures say about that.

3:6 Now **we command you, brethren, in the name of our Lord Jesus Christ, that ye withdraw yourselves from every brother that walketh disorderly, and not after the tradition** [doctrines of Holy Scripture] **which he received of us.**

Because our corporate church organizations refuse to reject the spiritually unclean and even welcome them; the time is coming when the faithful MUST withdraw themselves from the spiritually unclean organizations, polluted by compromise and tolerance for sin.

3:7 For yourselves know how ye ought to follow us: for we behaved not ourselves disorderly among you; **3:8** Neither did we eat any man's bread for nought; but wrought with labour and travail night and day, that we might not be chargeable to any of you: **3:9** Not because we have not power, but to make ourselves an ensample unto you to follow us. **3:10** For even when we were with you, this we commanded you, **that if any would not work, neither should he eat.**

Paul condemns the physically and spiritually lazy; saying that all should work physically for their own livelihood. How much more should we then labor for our spiritual daily bread?

3:11 For we hear that there are some which walk among you disorderly, working not at all, but are busybodies. **3:12** Now them that are such we command and exhort by our Lord Jesus Christ, that with quietness they work, and eat their own bread.

3:13 But ye, brethren, **be not weary in well doing** [do not be slack in zeal for keeping the whole Word of God].

We are to note and avoid all those who are not zealous to learn and to live by every Word of God.

3:14 And **if any man obey not our word by this epistle, note that man, and have no company with him, that he may be ashamed. 3:15** Yet count him not as an enemy, but admonish him as a brother.

We have peace with God through keeping God's Word and rejecting all sin and by doing God's Will; and by doing those things that are pleasing to God!

3:16 Now the Lord of peace himself give you peace always by all means. The Lord be with you all.

3:17 The salutation of Paul with mine own hand, which is the token in every epistle: so I write.

3:18 The grace of our Lord Jesus Christ be with you all. Amen.

First Timothy

1 Timothy 1

Paul's letters to Timothy and Titus give us instructions and qualifications for the ministry. A very large number of today's ministers have been inappropriately ordained contrary to the scripturally required qualifications, which is a main cause of the doctrinal drifting and accelerating apostasy of the past decades.

Every converted person has been called to become priests of our God, making this a very important subject. The books of Timothy and Titus teach us what WE ALL must do and how we must ALL live; to qualify as Kings and Priests and enter into the resurrection to eternal life.

> **Revelation 1:6** And **hath made us kings and priests unto God and his Father**; to him be glory and dominion for ever and ever. Amen.

The beginning of First Timothy has to do with the marriage relationship between a man and a women as an allegory of the relationship that Jesus Christ wants with his called out bride, and then leads into the qualifications for the ministry.

Paul identifies himself as an apostle which I am sure Timothy already knew.

1 Timothy 1:1 Paul, an apostle of Jesus Christ by the commandment of God our Saviour, and Lord Jesus Christ, which is our hope; **1:2** Unto Timothy, my own son in the faith: Grace, mercy, and peace, from God our Father and Jesus Christ our Lord.

At the very beginning of this Epistle Paul reminds Timothy and all elders throughout the ages, that their principle duty to teach all people to zealously live by every Word of God and to set an example of doing so.

1:3 As I besought thee to abide still at Ephesus, when I went into Macedonia, **that thou mightest charge** [command] some [the elders and teachers] that they teach no other doctrine [than the whole Word of God], **1:4** Neither give heed to fables [false teachings] and endless genealogies, which minister questions [contentions], rather than godly edifying [building up in godliness, which is the whole Word of God] which is in faith: so do.

1:5 Now the end of the commandment is charity [Godly love, which is the keeping of every Word of God in enthusiastic zeal.] out of a pure heart [Genuine godliness is the works of faith, and not the pretense of mere lip service like we see in today's Ekklesia.], and of a good conscience, and of faith unfeigned:

Then as today, many desire to be teachers and leaders without proper qualifications, not really understanding the sound doctrine of the whole Word of God. They think that they are teaching the truth, not realizing that they are in gross error from the scriptures.

1:6 From which some having swerved have turned aside unto vain jangling [Many having turned aside from the whole Word of God to empty words of false traditions and their own imaginations.]; **1:7** Desiring to be teachers of the law; understanding neither what they say, nor whereof they affirm.

Paul declares that the law of God is GOOD, but must be used lawfully; that is, the law must be kept in the manner that we are commanded to keep it. For example calling the Sabbath and High Days HOLY, which is the law is good; and then not keeping them according to God's instructions regarding HOW to keep them is unlawful.

1:8 But we know that the law is good, if a man use it lawfully;

The righteous man has the law written on his heart and mind, according to the New Covenant of Jeremiah 31:31. Yes, we need to study to fully learn and live by the Word of God, and the truth of the Word of God is revealed through patient diligent study and following the lead of the Holy Spirit of truth.

The law has no penalty and contains no threat to those who keep it, while the law is a threat to all those who break it.

If we stop at a stop light there is no fear of a ticket, but if we run a red light, then a penalty enters in. So it is with God's Word; if we love and keep God's Word there is no fear but rather the promise of eternal life; and if we break God's Word and law, there is a penalty attached, which is eternal death.

1:9 Knowing this, that the law is not made for a righteous man, but for the lawless and disobedient, for [The law was made and exists to restrain wickedness.] the ungodly and for sinners, for unholy and profane [Anyone who compromise with, or turns aside from any zeal to learn and to live by every Word of God in profane.], for murderers of fathers and murderers of mothers, for manslayers, **1:10** For whoremongers, for them that defile themselves with mankind [homosexuals], for menstealers, for liars [Liars include false teachers, and those who use and twist a small part of a larger truth to deceive about the larger truth.], for perjured [perjuring] persons, and if there be any other thing that is contrary to sound doctrine [God's Word condemns anything which is contrary to the sound doctrine of the whole Word of God.]; **1:11** According to the glorious gospel of [The true Gospel is the whole Word of God and not just some part of the scriptures.] the blessed God, which was committed to my trust.

Now the concept of God the Father's call to sincere repentance is brought in, as Paul explains that he a sinner who was called by God, to come to God the Father through Jesus Christ.

1:12 And I thank Christ Jesus our Lord, who hath enabled me, for that he counted me faithful, putting me into the ministry; **1:13** Who was before a blasphemer, and a persecutor, and injurious: but I obtained mercy, because I did it ignorantly in unbelief.

No man understands or believes God until he is called out of sin by God the Father and called to espousal with the Son, then his mind is opened to the wonders of God.

God's calling to godliness is by the Grace of God!

Grace is not permission to continue in sin; Grace is a calling out from and deliverance from bondage to sin!

1:14 And the grace of our Lord was exceeding abundant with faith and love which is in Christ Jesus. **1:15** This is a faithful saying, and worthy of all acceptation, that Christ Jesus came into the world to save sinners; of whom I am chief.

Paul tells us that God extended the Grace [Mercy] of God to him despite his wickedness, as an example that every sinner no matter how wicked, may also obtain mercy in their proper time through God's calling.

1:16 Howbeit for this cause I obtained [received] mercy, that in me first Jesus Christ might shew forth all longsuffering, **for a pattern to them which should hereafter believe on him to life everlasting.**

1:17 Now unto the King eternal, immortal, invisible, the only wise God, be honour and glory for ever and ever. Amen.

Paul then makes the point that he had put two persons out of the assembly because of unrepented blasphemy, proving that no willful sin is to be tolerated in our assemblies.

He commands Timothy and all future elders, leaders and teachers to have faith coupled with the works of faith, and to live in good conscience keeping the whole Word of God.

1:18 This charge I commit unto thee, son Timothy, according to the prophecies which went before on thee, that thou by them mightest war a good warfare; **1:19** Holding faith, and a good conscience; which some having put away concerning faith have made shipwreck: **1:20** Of whom is Hymenaeus and Alexander; whom I have delivered unto Satan, that they may learn not to blaspheme.

1 Timothy 2

Paul admonishes us to pray for all men [including our enemies]. This is often misunderstood as praying for their physical blessing, when we are really to pray that they will sincerely repent and turn towards godly conduct, or at least be peaceable towards the godly.

1 Timothy 2:1 I exhort therefore, that, first of all, supplications, prayers, intercessions, and giving of thanks, be made for all men; **2:2** For kings, and for all that are in authority [Pray for rulers that they do not persecute us by making laws attempting to force us to do anything contrary to God's Word.]; that we may lead a quiet and peaceable life in all godliness and honesty.

We are to pray for all people that they come to a knowledge of the truth and of godliness.

When we are persecuted; do not pay "Get this fellow," rather pray in a forgiving and loving attitude, asking God to forgive them and to open their eyes to what they are doing and to the truth, and lead them into sincere repentance and godliness.

Pray for all people as you would pray for a beloved child that has gone astray.

2:3 For this is good and acceptable in the sight of God our Saviour; **2:4** Who will have all men to be saved, and to come unto the knowledge of the truth.

2:5 For there is one God [the Father], and one mediator between God [the Father] and men, the man Christ Jesus;

The one who became Jesus Christ gave up his Godhood and as a physical man came and gave his life for us, after which he was resurrected to spirit and returned to God-hood as the ONLY Intercessor between God the Father and humanity.

2:6 Who gave himself a ransom for all, to be testified in due time.

Paul's calling was not by men; and his ministry was not by any ordination of men.

2:7 Whereunto I am ordained a preacher, and an apostle, (I speak the truth in Christ, and lie not;) a teacher of the Gentiles in faith and verity.

Paul commands as a part of Holy Scripture that we should put aside all hatred and pray for the good of all people. Remember the words of Christ as he was about to die, and also remember the words of Stephen as he was ready to die. "Forgive them for they know not what they do."

2:8 I will therefore that men pray every where, lifting up holy hands, **without wrath and doubting.**

Women are instructed to avoid seductive proud dress and personal appearance, and instead of spending hours on hair and makeup to spend their time on godly works.

This does not mean that women should not look their best, it means that moderation is needed in such things as makeup. In fact, overdoing makeup tends to detract from natural beauty; and is a measure of pride and vanity [they do not call makeup the vanity industry for nothing].

Nowhere do the scriptures condemn makeup, but Paul and the principles of scripture do insist on moderation. I suggest that it is not appropriate for anyone to spend more time on makeup and hair than they do on bible study or prayer. It is also wrong to dress so as to tease and tempt men.

2:9 In like manner also, that women adorn themselves in modest apparel, with shamefacedness and sobriety; not with broided hair, or gold, or pearls, or costly array; **2:10 But (which becometh women professing godliness) with good works.**

Women are to be silent and not interrupt the formal assemblies, and at home they are not to be contentious arguers, or to be constantly nagging like a continual dripping. They are to show proper respect for their men, both in and outside the formal services.

2:11 Let the woman learn in silence with all subjection. **2:12** But I suffer not a woman to teach [to teach men in the formal services, because it usurps the authority of the men (Ex 28:1,)], nor to usurp authority over the man, but to be in silence. **2:13** For Adam was first formed, then Eve. **2:14** And Adam was not deceived, but the woman being deceived was in the transgression.

Women will be saved by obeying God, just as the men are to obey God. God has ordained that the woman be subject to and be a help for her husband (Gen 3:16). The reason for this arrangement is so that the woman who led the man in rebellion in the garden, could learn obedience; while the man who followed the woman and not God, could learn to follow God.

To reject their God assigned roles is to reject the Word of God and to earn the reward of sin. To fulfill a wife's God assigned role and to be a strong support [in the Lord] for her husband; brings salvation [as long as she also keeps all the other things in God's Word]. Beyond that, just as death came into the world by a woman, so by the childbearing of women, life is continued in the physical world

2:15 Notwithstanding **she shall be saved in childbearing, if they continue in faith and charity** [if they continue in the love of God which is to live by every Word of God (1 Joh 2:5)] **and holiness** [which is the keeping of the whole Word of God] **with sobriety** [living in moderation].

1 Timothy 3

The term bishop was chosen by the translators according to their religious experience in 1611 and properly means elder. There is nothing wrong with desiring to be an elder as we are all called to become the priests of God in the resurrection. An elder in the biblical sense is simply one who is older in the faith and well experienced in life so that he is able to help his brothers and sisters.

Older brethren who meet these standards and who are manifestly already ordained by God, being well known for their godly wisdom and passionate zeal for the whole Word of God, are to be set apart and made known to the brethren by public ordination.

Nearly all of today's elders were ordained improperly as children [under the scriptural minimum age of 30 years for ordination (Num 4, and Luk 3:23)]; and were ordained not for any godliness but for other reasons including loyalty to men and corporate entities in place of any loyalty to God.

1 Timothy 3:1 This is a true saying, If a man desire the office of a bishop [an elder], he desireth a good work.

These qualifications are most easily understood in the physical realm, but each one also has its spiritual counterpart.

3:2 A bishop then must be blameless [in keeping God's Word], the husband of one wife [Must be or have been married to one wife at some time if widowed, and must be absolutely faithful to his one (at a time) wife.], vigilant [against all sin], sober [be spiritually awake and of a sound mind and of good judgment], of good behavior [living by every Word of God], given to hospitality [friendly and helpful to other brethren], apt to teach; **3:3** Not given to wine [not addicted to anything], no striker [not given to bullying others], not greedy of filthy lucre; but patient, not a brawler [not aggressive or contentious], not covetous [of position or anything else];

3:4 One that ruleth well his own house, having his children in subjection with all gravity [must have a full experience of raising children]; **3:5** (For if a man know not how to rule his own house, how shall he take care of the church of God?)

3:6 Not a novice [An elder must be spiritually mature, fully grounded on every Word of God and have proven himself to be a godly person over an extended time of years.], lest being lifted up with pride he fall into the condemnation of the devil.

3:7 Moreover he must have a good report of them which are without; lest he fall into reproach and the snare of the devil.

Deacons

3:8 Likewise must the deacons be grave, not doubletongued [sayng one thing to one person and saying another thing to another person], not given to much wine, not greedy of filthy lucre; **3:9** Holding the mystery of the faith in a pure conscience [being absolutely faithful to live by every Word of God].

3:10 And let these also first be proved [tested over time]; then let them use the office of a deacon, being found blameless. **3:11** Even so must their wives be grave, not slanderers, sober, faithful in all things.

3:12 Let the deacons be the husbands of [only] one wife, ruling their children and their own houses well.

3:13 For they that have used the office of a deacon well purchase to themselves a good degree, and great boldness in the faith which is in Christ Jesus.

3:14 These things write I unto thee, hoping to come unto thee shortly: **3:15** But if I tarry [delay] long, that thou mayest know how thou oughtest to behave thyself in the house of God [the spiritual Ekklesia], which is the church [the Ekklesia, the brotherhood, the family] of the living God, the pillar and ground of the truth.

There can be no argument that the wonders of the scriptures are impossible to understand by the mind of man. The Word, plan and mind of God is so absolutely incredibly awesome!

3:16 And without controversy great is the mystery of godliness: God was manifest in the flesh [the Creator gave up his Godhood to be made flesh], justified in the Spirit, seen of angels, preached unto the Gentiles [Jesus preached to the Samaritans and Phoenicians and the Romans and Greeks in Judea as well as to the Jews.], believed on in the world, received up [was resurrected back to God-hood] into glory.

Brethren, nearly ALL of today's church leaders and most of the elders were wrongfully ordained by men, not meeting the scriptural requirements for ordination.

This is one of the root causes of today's pathetic Laodicean situation. The brethren follow men and not God, and their leaders and elders follow human idols and not God. Their Shining Light of godly example has flickered out.

The answer is in plain sight. We have let our Light of godly example go out, becoming just another one of many mainstream churches while adding a pretense of the Sabbath.

The answer is to turn to a passionate zeal to please Almighty God and to live by every Word of God.

Hear the Word of the LORD!
Isaiah 56

> The vast majority of today's spiritual Ekklesia call the Sabbath holy; and then they regularly pollute it by cooking, going to restaurants and otherwise working or paying others to work on the Sabbath.

The neglect of the sanctity of the Sabbath was a major reason why God sent Israel into captivity in the past and it is a major reason why Jesus Christ will reject the latter day church of God groups and cast them into the correction of great tribulation.

We have NO zeal for the teachings and commandments of Holy Scripture and instead stand on our false traditions. We water down the scriptures on the Sabbath and we reject the scriptures in favor of the false teachings of mere mortal men.

> **Nehemiah 10:31** And if the people of the land bring ware or any **victuals** on the sabbath day to sell, that **we would not buy it of them on the sabbath, or on the holy day**: and that we would leave the seventh year, and the exaction of every debt.

We are commended to keep the judgments and to live by every Word of Holy Scripture; which define and are the righteousness of God in print. We are called to learn and to keep the letter and the spirit and intent of the entire body of scripture.

Isaiah 56:1 Thus saith the LORD, Keep ye judgment, and do justice: for my salvation is near to come, and my righteousness to be revealed.

Blessed are those who repent and are zealous to learn and keep every Word of Holy Scripture; and blessed are those who are zealous for the Holy Seventh Day [Fri sunset to Sat sunset] Sabbath; commanded at creation by our Creator.

56:2 Blessed is the man that doeth this, and the son of man that layeth hold on it; that keepeth the sabbath from polluting it, and keepeth his hand from doing any evil.

Love and zeal for the sanctity of the Sabbath is the first step on the road to salvation for it gives us a time to learn about our Maker and a time to study his Word; it indicates to God the Father and to Jesus Christ, how much we love them.

Those who lose jobs, friends, family and physical comfort and wealth because of their zeal for God's Sabbath will receive great blessings from God including eternal life.

Those who like Esau are willing to sell the birthright of their calling for the physical pleasures of this world and who STEAL God's time to use as they want, will fall into great correction and if they will not repent they will fall into destruction of the spirit as well as the flesh.

Zeal for God's Sabbath brings us close to God as we take the time to study and learn of him on HIS time.

56:3 Neither let the son of the stranger, that hath joined himself to the LORD, speak, saying, The LORD hath utterly separated me from his people: neither let the eunuch say, Behold, I am a dry tree.

The physical eunuch is used as a type of those who are ostracized from others because of their zeal for the Sabbath and all the holy scriptures; because they are zealous for God the Father and Jesus Christ, and not for the false ways of human leaders who water down doctrine and pollute the Sabbath.

Those who are ostracized for their zeal for God will find themselves being given eternal life with many, many, others, who are also zealous and they will all be a part of the Family of God.

56:4 For thus saith the LORD unto the eunuchs that keep my sabbaths, and choose the things that please me, and take hold of my covenant; **56:5** Even unto them will I give in mine house [God's Family] and within my walls a place and a name better than of sons and of daughters: I will give them an everlasting name, that shall not be cut off.

The promise is to Israel and also to the Gentiles who are zealous to live by every Word of God and who maintain the sanctity of the Holy Seventh Day Sabbath [Fri sunset to Sat sunset].

Zeal for God's Sabbath is a sign of both the Mosaic and the New Covenants: Those who lack zeal for the sanctity of the Sabbath, lack zeal for their covenant relationship with God the Father and Jesus Christ.

56:6 Also the sons of the stranger, that join themselves to the LORD, to serve him, and to love the name of the LORD, to be his servants, every one that keepeth the sabbath from polluting it, and taketh hold of my covenant;

The zealous for the teachings, commandments and Holy Sabbath, for every Word of God; will be accepted by God the Father and will be welcomed in the House [the spiritual temple, the family] of God.

56:7 Even them will I bring to my holy mountain, and make them joyful in my house of prayer: their burnt offerings and their sacrifices shall be accepted upon mine altar; **for mine house shall be called an house of prayer for all people.**

When Jesus Christ comes and gathers together the outcasts of Israel to himself, he will also gather the Gentiles to him; for all the earth will repent (Is 60:3, Zech 14:16) and turn to zeal for all the Teachings, Commandments, Word and Will of God; and to a zeal for his Holy Sabbath Day!

56:8 The Lord GOD, which gathereth the outcasts of Israel saith, Yet will I gather others to him, beside those that are gathered unto him.

Because we call the Sabbath holy and pollute it; because we have no zeal for the ways of God and yet we are filled with zeal for our idols of men and organizations who teach us to depart from zeal for the Word of God; We will be rejected by Jesus Christ (Rev 3:14-22) and thrust into the fiery furnace of correction.

The beasts of the forest and the beasts of the field, represent the nations of the Gentiles

56:9 All ye beasts of the field, come to devour, yea, all ye beasts in the forest.

The leaders of today's physical nations of Israel are ignorant of the things of righteousness; and the watchmen, leaders and elders of spiritual Israel are spiritually blind; they are asleep and not giving the warning.

Yes, they speak of prophecy but without understanding, because they will not live by every Word of God the Father and Jesus Christ. They have been given over to spiritual slumber because they have no zeal to live by every Word of God.

56:10 His watchmen are blind: they are all ignorant, they are all dumb dogs, they cannot bark; sleeping, lying down, loving to slumber.

The leaders of today's spiritual Ekklesia are like greedy dogs each doing his own thing and never being satisfied with what they are demanding. They water down the Sabbath and the sound doctrine of Holy Scripture to try to attract personal followers.

A good understanding is withheld from them because of their lack of zeal for God's Sabbath and for living by every Word of God the Father.

56:11 Yea, they are greedy dogs which can never have enough, and they are shepherds that cannot understand: they all look to their own way, every one for his gain, from his quarter.

They fill themselves with the strong drink of their own imaginations, and become intoxicated with pride in their own ways.

They say the end is near, to extort income; while they really believe that "My Lord delays his coming." This is demonstrated by their grand construction projects.

56:12 Come ye, say they, I will fetch wine, and we will fill ourselves with strong drink; and to morrow shall be as this day, and much more abundant.

The Faithful have God's own promise that if we turn to him there is a blessing!

Isaiah 58:13 If thou turn away thy foot from the sabbath, from doing thy pleasure on my holy day; and call the sabbath a delight, the holy of the Lord, honourable; and shalt honour him, not doing thine own ways, nor finding thine own pleasure, nor speaking thine own words: **58:14** Then shalt thou delight thyself in the Lord; and I will cause thee to ride upon the high places of the earth, and feed thee with the heritage of Jacob thy father: for the mouth of the Lord hath spoken it.

1 Timothy 4

1 Timothy 4:1 Now the Spirit speaketh expressly, that **in the latter times some shall depart from the faith, giving heed to seducing spirits, and doctrines of devils; 4:2 Speaking lies in hypocrisy; having their conscience seared with a hot iron;**

This is being fulfilled in today's spiritual Ekklesia as they continue to water down and change doctrine away from the truth of God's Word and also reject any increase in a sound understanding of the truth. Then they teach that one need not and should not be zealous to live by every Word of God or to keep the Sabbath as the scriptures command; teaching people to blindly follow idols of men, and teaching many other falsehoods.

4:3 Forbidding to marry, and **commanding to abstain from meats [vegetarian], which God hath created to be received with thanksgiving of them which believe and know the truth**. [Eating meat sanctified by the Word of God; that is, eating scripturally clean meats is lawful.] **4:4** For every creature of God is good, and nothing to be refused, **if it be received with thanksgiving: 4:5 For it is sanctified by** [The meat that we eat must be from those creatures which are sanctified by the Word of God (Deu 14, Lev 11).] **the word of God and prayer.**

Leviticus 11 reveals what has been sanctified by God for human consumption and what is forbidden. Many have tried to put this in terms of what is physically good for us and what is not; when the real purpose of setting apart the clean from the unclean is to teach us to make a difference between the holy and the profane (Lev 10:10).

4:6 If thou put the brethren in remembrance of these things, thou shalt be a good minister of Jesus Christ, nourished up in the words of faith and of good doctrine, whereunto thou hast attained.

4:7 But refuse profane [unholy things and false teachings] and old wives' fables [the false traditions of men], and exercise thyself rather unto godliness.

Work at learning and living by every Word of God.

Spiritually exercising the mind and spirit is far more profitable for the spirit than physical exercise is profitable for the physical body; therefore why exercise the body and neglect to exercise the spirit in prayer, study, thinking on godly things and living a godly life?

4:8 For bodily exercise profiteth little: but godliness is profitable unto all things, having promise of the life that now is, and of that which is to come.

Paul and Timothy both labored to help others towards godliness and were willing to suffer for their zeal for the whole Word of God; which is the duty of all elders AND brethren!

4:9 This is a faithful saying and worthy of all acceptation. **4:10** For therefore we both labour and suffer reproach, because we trust in the living God, who is the Saviour of all men, specially of those that believe.

4:11 These things command and teach.

The word "youth" is relative and does not mean that Timothy was a child. Men of 60 consider men of 45 to be youths. The sense of this is that there were people older than Timothy in the congregations, and that Timothy was to treat them with respect, but he was not to feel intimidated by them.

Now comes a partial list of the duties of an elder. They are to be Shining Lights of examples of zealous godliness

4:12 Let no man despise thy youth; but **be thou an example of the believers, in word, in conversation, in charity** [Godly love which is the keeping of the whole Word of God], **in spirit, in faith** [which includes the works of faith, which is a zealous keeping of God's Word], **in purity** [from all sin]. **4:13** Till I come [All subsequent elders are to do likewise until

Christ comes, and forever after that.], give attendance to reading [the scriptures], to exhortation [exhorting to zealously live by every Word of God], to doctrine [expounding the sound doctrine of the whole Word of God].

The called out are all called to be priests of God and we are not to neglect our calling and the gifts of God's Spirit. The elders, leaders and all of the brethren in the Ekklesia are not to neglect spiritual things, but we are to exercise ourselves spiritually towards true passionate godliness.

4:14 Neglect not the gift that is in thee, which was given thee by prophecy, with the laying on of the hands of the presbytery [the congregation, the brethren] .

4:15 Meditate [think deeply] upon these things; **give thyself wholly to them** [we must dedicate ourselves to wholehearted godliness]; that thy profiting [So that our spiritual growth is known to all; this instruction is for us also and our spiritual growth should be a Shining Example of godliness for all people.] may appear to all.

4:16 Take heed unto thyself [to remain zealous and faithful to God], and unto the doctrine [the sound doctrine of the whole Word of God]; continue in them: for in doing this thou shalt both save thyself, and them that hear thee.

Once called, repenting and having Christ's sacrifice applied to us we will be saved by our zeal for godliness and our zeal to internalize the whole Word of God, so that we become of ONE mind and ONE spirit with God the Almighty..

1 Timothy 5

Instructions on how elders are to treat the brethren. For many years this instruction about elders has been misapplied to falsely insist that no minister is to be rebuked for their sins.

The context in this verse concerns age and has nothing to do with some office in the assembly. Paul is forbidding bullying and is instructing the ministry to treat older people with the respect and honor due to parents, to treat the younger men as their own brothers, to treat older women as if they were our mothers and to treat the younger women as if they were our own sisters.

1 Timothy 5:1 Rebuke not an elder [do not bully an older person, or any person], but intreat him [with the respect due a father] as a father; and the younger men as brethren; **5:2** The elder women as mothers; the younger as sisters, with all purity.

Take care of the true widow who is completely alone; but those who have family, let their own families help take care of their relatives and live a godly life, and not be a burden to the Ekklesia. This is also an instruction regarding spiritual widows. If any spiritual widow [whose husband has abandoned her] has relatives in the faith, they and their relatives should care for each other and not burden the Ekklesia.

5:3 Honour widows that are widows indeed. **5:4** But if any widow have children or nephews, let them learn first to shew piety at home, and to requite [care for] their parents: for that is good and acceptable before God.

A true godly widow has no help but places all her trust in God; dedicating herself to please God and to the godly serving of others.

But if a widow [or a man] is wanton and living in the pleasures and lusts of worldliness; they are spiritually dead even if they are physically alive.

5:5 Now she that is a widow indeed, and desolate, trusteth in God, and continueth in supplications and prayers night and day. **5:6** But she that liveth in pleasure is dead while she liveth. **5:7** And these things give in charge, that they may be blameless.

In this context we are commanded to provide for our own families including our widows, and our widows are commanded to be a help for their physical relatives in the faith and also help their spiritual relatives.

The concept is that widows are not to be a burden to the community of faith [in other words no one is to unnecessarily burden others] while being lazy and wanton, but they are to serve in any way they can; while those who are related to widows are to help and provide for those widows so that the assembly is not unduly burdened.

The following also concerns those who mistakenly give large offerings while neglecting the needs of the wives, parents and children that God has blessed us with.

We are NOT to give to the organization until it hurts! We are to fulfill the responsibilities that Almighty God has given us in regards to our families first, before making any voluntary offering. I am referring to voluntary offerings here.

We are to properly care for the family that God has blessed us with.

5:8 But **if any provide not for his own, and specially for those of his own house, he hath denied the faith, and is worse than an infidel.**

To be supported by the Ekklesia a widow must have been the wife of only one man [in other words not having been wanton with many men] and must be at least 60, the inference being that she could not be expected to earn her own living after the age of 60. It should be self-evident that a younger widow with health problems or with young children should also be cared for.

5:9 Let not a widow be taken into the number under threescore years old, having been the wife of one man.

Paul outlines some of the good works of faith expected from widows. A woman who is destitute and supported by the Ekklesia is not to sit about in idleness. She is to visit the sick, encourage and teach the younger women, care for others and generally be a Shining Light of godly service and example; while diligently studying and living by every Word of God. Our older women have very much to offer and can be a huge help in the Ekklesia.

Every person has their own gifts and all should exercise those gifts in service to the brethren, to the edifying and building up of the whole body; even the aged who can do nothing physically can still labor in prayer and wise advice.

5:10 Well reported of for good works; if she have brought up children, if she have lodged strangers, if she have washed the saints' feet, if she have relieved the afflicted, if she have diligently followed every good work.

Reject supporting any younger widows who have not yet proven to be trustworthy in godliness and are idle busybodies; not being zealous to live and serve in godliness.

This means that strong young women [able to work and care for themselves] who go about in idleness and do not serve the Ekklesia in godliness should not be supported by the brethren; they should work and support themselves. The Ekklesia need not support the idle lazy, the widows are to work and contribute for their own support if they can, and are not to be idle and lazy. Obviously those who are aged, ill, handicapped or with young children would be exceptions.

This principle applies to men as well. Men should work and not be a burden to the Ekklesia; even handicapped men can do something, at least spending their time in study and encouraging others.

5:11 But the younger widows refuse: for when they have begun to wax wanton against Christ, they will marry [outside the faith]; **5:12** Having damnation, because they have cast off their first faith. **5:13** And withal they learn to be idle, wandering about from house to house; and not only idle, but tattlers also and busybodies, speaking things which they ought not.

Paul recommends that younger women marry.

Some have mistakenly thought that Paul recommends that people not marry; that is an erroneous idea. Paul recommended that some not marry because of the circumstances of severe trials they were going through in that particular area; but overall it is God's will from the very beginning; that we marry.

5:14 I will therefore that the younger women marry, bear children, guide the house, give none occasion to the adversary to speak reproachfully. **5:15** For some are already turned aside after Satan.

Here Paul comes to the point: We are to care for our own and we are not to expect others to fulfill our family responsibilities for us.

5:16 If any man or woman that believeth have widows, let them relieve them, and let not the church be charged; **that it may relieve them that are widows indeed.**

Those elders who labor in the sound doctrine of the whole Word of God are to be honored. The term "honor" is a reference to respecting, supporting and providing for those who work for your spiritual growth and bring to you the words of salvation. This does NOT mean that mere mortals are to be idolized and blindly followed; they are to be honored only as long as they are faithful to every Word of God.

5:17 Let the elders that rule well be counted worthy of double honour, **especially they who labour in the word and doctrine. 5:18** For the scripture saith, Thou shalt not muzzle the ox that treadeth out the corn. And, The labourer is worthy of his reward.

Paul teaches that at least two witness (Deu 17:6, 19:15) are needed to establish the guilt of an elder. In fact the law requires at least two or three witnesses to establish any matter. This requires witnesses to the actual event, hearsay and rumor are not to be accepted; nor are half truths and spin.

5:19 Against an elder receive not an accusation, but before two or three witnesses.

> **Deuteronomy 19:15** One witness shall not rise up against a man for any iniquity, or for any sin, in any sin that he sinneth: at the mouth of two witnesses, or at the mouth of three witnesses, shall the matter be established.

1 Timothy 5:20 Them [speaking of elders but referring to all willful sinners] that sin **rebuke before all, that others also may fear. 5:21** I charge thee before God, and the Lord Jesus Christ, and the elect angels, **that thou observe these things without preferring one before another, doing nothing by partiality.**

Of course most churches do not follow this instruction to rebuke sinning elders before all.

Many of them are also infamous for taking a tiny fraction of a larger truth and spinning it to appear to mean the opposite of what it does mean in its proper context; which is deceiving and bearing false witness.

No person is to be ordained without a long experience in the faith, being at least 30 years old (Num 4, Luk 3:23) having much good fruit in zeal for the whole Word of God.

We are not to be partakers [to participate in, or delight to watch] of the sins of others; for example associating with drunkards, watching porn, or eating in restaurants on the Sabbath, or going to another person's home for a big meal on the Sabbath.

5:22 Lay hands suddenly on no man, neither be partaker of other men's sins: keep thyself pure.

This is a personal matter for Timothy to take a LITTLE bit his apparent bad health and is not an instruction for us to become wine bibbers.

5:23 Drink no longer water, but use a little wine for thy stomach's sake and thine often infirmities.

The sins or good works of some are obvious, while in other cases they may not be known until much later.

5:24 Some men's sins are open beforehand, going before to judgment; and some men they follow after. **5:25** Likewise also the good works of some are manifest beforehand; and they that are otherwise cannot be hid.

1 Timothy 6

1 Timothy 6:1 Let as many servants as are under the yoke count their own masters worthy of all honour, that the name of God and his doctrine be not blasphemed.

Those who find themselves servants [and employees] should serve with respect for the authority of their employers; setting a godly example for all people.

6:2 And they that have believing masters, let them not despise them, because they are brethren; but rather do them service, because they are faithful and beloved, partakers of the benefit. These things teach and exhort.

This is a powerful condemnation of today's elders and leaders who teach people to follow idols of men, corporate entities and false traditions; and teach to reject any zeal to learn and to keep the whole Word of God.

6:3 If any man teach otherwise [contrary to the scriptures], and consent not to wholesome words [of scripture], **even the words of our Lord Jesus Christ, and to the doctrine which is according to godliness** [the whole Word of God]; **6:4** He is proud, knowing nothing, but doting about questions and strifes of words, whereof cometh envy, strife, railings, evil surmisings, **6:5** Perverse disputings of men of corrupt minds, and destitute of the truth, supposing that gain is godliness: from such withdraw thyself.

6:6 But godliness [living by every Word of God] with contentment [not lusting after physical gain] is great gain. **6:7** For we brought nothing into this world, and it is certain we can carry nothing out. **6:8** And having food and raiment let us be therewith content.

Pursue after godly things which are eternal and do not covet after physical riches which are vanity and disappearing mist. Many have compromised with the pursuit of godliness when seeking physical gain.

We see this tragedy with those who compromise with sound doctrine and turn aside from any zeal to obey God in exchange for the hope of physical gain.

6:9 But they that will be rich fall into temptation and a snare, and into many foolish and hurtful lusts, which drown men in destruction and perdition. **6:10** For the love of money is the root of all evil: which while some coveted after [Many are willing to compromise for gain, and have erred from sound doctrine for the hope of money, respect from men and followers.], **they have erred from the faith, and pierced themselves through with many sorrows.**

Godly people are to flee covetousness [unlawful desires] and the watering down of doctrine.

6:11 But thou, O man of God, flee these things; and follow after righteousness, godliness, faith, love, patience, meekness.

ALL Godly people both men and women, are to fight the good fight for the whole Word of God and we must never compromise with our zeal to live by every Word of God.

6:12 Fight the good fight of faith, lay hold on eternal life, whereunto thou art also called, [We are to be a LIGHT of godly example; Shining an example of zealous godliness brightly before all.] and hast professed a good profession before many witnesses.

Paul commands Timothy and through him the whole people of God, to be zealous to live by every Word of God far above any concern for worldly things. As also Wisdom saith.

> **Proverbs 8:11** For wisdom is better than rubies; and all the things that may be desired are not to be compared to it.

1 Timothy 6:13 I give thee charge in the sight of God, who quickeneth all things, and before Christ Jesus, who before Pontius Pilate witnessed a good confession; **6:14 That thou keep this commandment without spot,**

unrebukable, until the appearing of our Lord Jesus Christ: **6:15** Which in his times he shall shew, who is the blessed and only Potentate, the King of kings, and Lord of lords; **6:16** Who only hath immortality, dwelling in the light which no man can approach unto; whom no man hath seen, nor can see: to whom be honour and power everlasting. Amen.

6:17 Charge them that are rich in this world, that they be not highminded [proud because of physical possessions and supposed knowledge], **nor trust in uncertain riches, but** [trust] **in the living God,** who giveth us richly all things to enjoy;

6:18 That they [we should not be proud but should] do good, that they be rich in good works, ready to distribute, willing to communicate [God's Word]; **6:19** Laying up in store for themselves a good foundation against the time to come [laying up a spiritual reward in heaven], that they may lay hold on eternal life.

> **Matthew 6:19-21** Lay not up for yourselves treasures upon earth, where **moth** and rust doth corrupt, and where thieves break through and steal: But lay up for yourselves treasures in heaven, where neither **moth** nor rust doth corrupt, and where thieves do not break through nor steal: For where your treasure is, there will your heart be also.

This instruction to Timothy is, by being recorded as Holy Scripture; also an instruction to all of God's people wherever and whenever they live.

1 Timothy 6:20 O Timothy, keep that which is committed to thy trust [the Word of God], avoiding profane and vain babblings, and oppositions of science falsely so called: **6:21** Which some professing have erred concerning the faith. Grace be with thee. Amen.

Second Timothy

2 Timothy 1

While this letter is addressed to Timothy, by virtue of its being recorded and preserved as Holy Scripture it is applicable to all of the called out today.

2 Timothy 1:1 Paul, an apostle of Jesus Christ by the will of God, according to the promise of life which is in Christ Jesus, **1:2** To Timothy, my dearly beloved son: Grace, mercy, and peace, from God the Father and Christ Jesus our Lord.

Timothy was taught godliness by his mother and grandmother.

We are to diligently teach a passionate zeal for the whole Word of God to our children, and if they are not called now they will still be well prepared for their future calling.

This does not mean that we are to be brutal bullies trying to beat godliness into them, it means that from the moment of birth we are to bond with them, to spend much loving affectionate time with them, constantly ENCOURAGING them towards what is right; and to patiently teach them the way that they should go.

1:3 I thank God, whom I serve from my forefathers [Paul also came from a family who had zealously served God to the best of their understanding;

Paul being taught a zeal for God by his parents and forbearers.] with pure conscience, that without ceasing I have remembrance of thee [Paul payed for Timothy and we should pray for our own families and for others, that God would open their understanding to his Word.] in my prayers night and day; **1:4** Greatly desiring to see thee, being mindful of thy tears, that I may be filled with joy; **1:5** When I call to remembrance the unfeigned faith that is in thee, which dwelt first in thy grandmother Lois, and thy mother Eunice; and I am persuaded that in thee also.

Paul said that after Timothy was ordained by the congregation, Paul also later laid hands on Timothy that he might receive the Holy Spirit.

Timothy is told to stir up, to exercise and use God's Spirit, which he had received as a gift from God; just as we all are to stir up God's gift of the Holy Spirit which we received at our sincere repentance and baptism.

1:6 Wherefore I put thee in remembrance that thou stir up the gift of God, which is in thee by the putting on of my hands.

God's Spirit is the Spirit of God the Father and Jesus Christ living in us, and it is the Spirit of power to overcome all evil just as Christ overcame.

The Holy Spirit is the Spirit of truth and godly love and a passionate love to learn and to live by every Word of God. It is the Spirit of a sound mind to understand and retain spiritual things and of power to control our sinful nature. God's Spirit is the very nature of God!

1:7 For God hath not given us the spirit of fear; but of power, and of love, and of a sound mind.

Be not ashamed to boldly declare and live by every Word of God!

In preaching, do not shrink back from declaring the whole Word of God; do NOT sinfully give way to an inoffensive Business Model Outreach. Do not compromise with or water down the truth of God into weak platitudes and mere words without the required works of faith!

1:8 Be not thou therefore ashamed of the testimony of our Lord, nor of me his prisoner: but be thou partaker of the afflictions of the gospel according to the power of God; **1:9** Who hath saved us, and called us with an holy calling, not according to our works, but according to his own purpose and grace, which was given us in Christ Jesus before the world began, **1:10** But is now made manifest by the [first] appearing of our Saviour Jesus Christ, who hath abolished death [Jesus Christ abolished the penalty of eternal death for sin for the sincerely repentant, by dying for us in our place.], and hath brought [the knowledge of eternal life] life and immortality to light through the gospel: **1:11** Whereunto I am appointed a preacher, and an apostle, and a teacher of the Gentiles.

Paul was not ashamed of Jesus Christ and neither should we be ashamed of the way to eternal life. Are we not willing to endure when our LORD suffered so much?

> **John 15:18** If the world hate you, ye know that it hated me before it hated you.
>
> **15:19** If ye were of the world, the world would love his own: but because ye are not of the world, but I have chosen you out of the world, therefore the world hateth you.
>
> **15:20** Remember the word that I said unto you, The servant is not greater than his lord. **If they have persecuted me, they will also persecute you**; if they have kept my saying, they will keep yours also.
>
> **15:21** But all these things will they do unto you for my name's sake, because they know not him that sent me.

We should KNOW that God the Father who raised up Jesus Christ because Jesus was not ashamed of the truth of the Father; will raise us up also, if we are not ashamed of the truth of God the Father and of the Son!

> **Matthew 10:32** Whosoever therefore shall confess me before men, him will I confess also before my Father which is in heaven.
>
> **10:33** But whosoever shall deny me before men, him will I also deny before my Father which is in heaven.
>
> **10:34** Think not that I am come to send peace on earth: I came not to send peace, but a sword.

Brethren, whoever compromises with the whole Word of God; IS, by denying the Word of God also denying God the Father and the Son!

2 Timothy 1:12 For the which cause I also suffer these things: nevertheless I am not ashamed: for I know whom I have believed, and am persuaded that he is able to keep that which I have committed unto him against that day.

We are to hold fast to the whole Word of God including the scriptural words of Paul.

1:13 Hold fast the form of **sound words** [the Holy Scriptures], which thou hast heard of me, in faith and love which is in Christ Jesus.

1:14 That good thing [the whole Word of God] which was committed unto thee keep by the Holy Ghost which dwelleth in us.

Very many have twisted the words of Paul into the exact opposite of their intended meaning in an attempt to justify continuing in sin. We see in these studies the true meaning of the words of Paul and we can now understand Paul's great zeal to learn and to keep the whole Word of God.

Even in Paul's day some of the called out were deceived and led astray and our Lord warned us that in these last days (Mat 24) that MANY false teachers will arise within the Ekklesia.

1:15 This thou knowest, that **all they which are in Asia be turned away from** me; of whom are Phygellus and Hermogenes.

Onesimus had fled his master Philemon's home to seek out Paul to learn more about God. He was a great help to Paul, but later Paul sent him back to his master with the Epistle of Philemon. It appears that his master Philemon then gave Onesimus permission to return to and help Paul.

1:16 The Lord give mercy unto the house of Onesiphorus [Onesimus of the books of Colossians and Philemon]; for he oft refreshed me, and was not ashamed of my chain: **1:17** But, when he was in [Philemon apparently gave his servant Onesimus consent to seek Paul in Rome] Rome, he sought me out very diligently, and found me.

1:18 The Lord grant unto him that he may find mercy of the Lord in that day [in the resurrection to spirit]: and in how many things he ministered unto me at Ephesus, thou [Timothy] knowest very well.

2 Timothy 2

Paul encourages Timothy to "Be Strong," to zealously learn and live by every Word of God, and to live by the Will of God the Father in all things. Brethren, let us all do likewise for God calls to us: "Be Strong and Persevere, My Son!"

2 Timothy 2:1 Thou therefore, my son, be strong in the grace [Be strong and diligent in our calling to repentance and reconciliation with God, to learn and to live by every Word of God and to teach all others to do likewise.] that is in Christ Jesus.

Paul tells Timothy to teach others, who would then be able to teach many more: the whole Word of God.

Today, God has provided the marvelous tool of the internet and many are being taught the sound doctrine of Holy Scripture, but it will not stop there; for many of these others will then teach many others in due time.

Do not despise the day of small beginnings for a small few will go to God's prepared place, but very many others will wake up and remember what they have heard as the Tribulation unfolds (at least 144,000, Rev 7); then they will be able to teach many others.

Brethren, this work is not merely about the coming correction of great tribulation; this work is about preparing and perfecting the spiritual bride for her wedding day!

2:2 And **the things that thou hast heard of me** among many witnesses, the **same commit thou to faithful men, who shall be able to teach others also.**

Paul's encouragement to endure extremely adverse conditions to obtain the tremendous results intended by Almighty God, are also to encourage each one of us to do our part as well!

Let us also be full of passionate zeal to pray, to diligently study, to think always on godliness, so that we may learn godliness and become a Shining Example of keeping God's Word, and that we may be prepared to teach the whole Word of God to all who seek it!

2:3 Thou therefore endure hardness, as a good soldier of Jesus Christ.

Let us not entangle ourselves with worldliness, but totally immerse ourselves in learning and living godliness, fighting a godly spiritual warfare against all sin and against the Adversary.

2:4 No man that warreth entangleth himself with the affairs of this life; that he may please him who hath chosen him to be a soldier.

Let us strive to master sin and to learn fully the whole Word of God, so that we may wield the sharp sword of the Spirit, which is the whole truth of Almighty God!

Let us strive for godliness, wholeheartedly with all that we are, and with all that God gives us, so that we may be a worthy part of the eternal collective bride of Christ!

2:5 And if a man also strive for masteries, yet is he not crowned, except he strive lawfully.

The laborer is worthy of his wages; but give what is appropriate to your personal responsibilities to the family that God has given you.

I do not mean for people to try to give every child a Ferrari while neglecting the Laborers of God; I mean to properly provide for genuine needs, and to pay our bills. Do not give a huge free will offering, when the family car is unsafe needing brakes! Use some godly sense and God's Spirit of sound judgment!

2:6 The husbandman that laboureth must be first partaker of the fruits.

Seek understanding from God in prayer, in addition to reading and thinking about God's Word. Ask God to reveal what he means in BOTH the letter and the spirit and intent of His Word.

2:7 Consider what I say; and **the Lord give thee understanding in all things**.

Remember that God the Father raised up Jesus Christ for his sinless zeal to live by every Word of, and the Will of God the Father; and that the Father will also raise us up to an eternal spirit life if we continue in Christ-like zeal for all the things of God the Father!

2:8 Remember that Jesus Christ of the seed of David was raised from the dead [for his sinless zeal for godliness] according to my gospel [Paul's teachings]:

Those who stand on and proclaim the truth of the whole Word of God will be persecuted by those who do not like what they hear and want to continue in their sins deciding right and wrong for themselves.

2:9 Wherein I suffer trouble, as an evil doer, even unto bonds; but the word of God is not bound [restrained].

The reward for following godliness is very great indeed, for we shall obtain the salvation of eternal life [Which is worth enduring for!]; and those who persecuted the godly in the past will ultimately have their minds opened and will then seek out those who they have abused to learn about godliness from them.

Today's enemies will become our greatest friends in future, for they will know what they have done, they will know how wrong they were and they will know how much they have been forgiven; they will sincerely repent and become filled with godly love themselves! That is WORTH enduring for!

2:10 Therefore I endure all things for the elect's sakes, that they may also obtain the salvation which is in Christ Jesus with eternal glory.

If we have destroyed our old man of sin to become a new person in Christ; we shall be raised up to eternal life as spirits, just as Christ was raised up to spirit and eternal life!

2:11 It is a faithful saying: For if we be dead with him, we shall also live with him:

If we endure sufferings as Christ endured sufferings, without any hint of compromise, spiritual idolatry or spiritual adultery; we will live and rule with Christ as a part of his bride!

As a bride is to be one with and partake of her husband's estate: If we faint not we will be united as one with Jesus Christ and shall partake of the bounty of Christ our Husband, to become rulers of nations under our King of kings; and to become priests of our High Priest of salvation, Jesus Christ (Rev 1:6, 5:10)!

2:12 If we suffer, we shall also reign with him: if we deny him, he also will deny us: **2:13** If we believe not, yet he abideth faithful: he cannot deny himself.

We are not to strive in splitting hairs on words and establishing a belief on the meaning of one word, we are to put all the scriptures together to arrive at the true sense of the teaching.

False teachers will take a word out of context, add their own definition to it and then spin an entire doctrine [teaching] around that supposition. That is the logic of Aristotle: The logic may be superb, yet one cannot reach a correct conclusion if the logic is based on a false premise [foundation].

Example: Teachers who claim and start with the premise that they are God's leaders; and then claim based on that premise, that we must obey them blindly and without question or without proving their words by God's Word.

If anyone accepts that they are God's appointed leaders and that to question them is rebellion against God; then they can with clever words lead the brethren into any sin at all.

Watch that premise: The truth is that if someone is a TRUE teacher of God, he would be subject to the Word of God and would not be teaching his own ways. People who reject God's Word for their own ways are false teachers; anyone who is not consistent with the whole Word of God is not a person of God.

2:14 Of these things put them in remembrance, charging them before the Lord that they strive not about words to no profit, but to the subverting of the hearers.

We are to be continual in our prayer and studies by constantly thinking about godliness day and night.

2:15 Study to shew thyself approved unto God, a workman that needeth not to be ashamed, rightly dividing the word of truth.

Be always ready to answer honest questions but avoid pointless and endless empty arguments with made up minds, which are only meant to create strife and waste the time of godly people.

2:16 But shun profane and vain babblings: for they will increase unto more ungodliness. **2:17** And their word will eat as doth a canker: of whom is Hymenaeus and Philetus; **2:18 Who concerning the truth have erred, saying that the resurrection is past already**; and overthrow the faith of some.

Let everyone who is in Christ depart from all sin and follow God the Father with Christ-like zeal.

Those who claim to be God's people and justify remaining in any sin; are LIARS and not of God!

Those who call the Sabbath day holy, and then pollute it by rejecting God's commandments on how to observe the Sabbath, or who reject the Biblical Calendar, or who reject any zeal for godliness: are NOT men of God! They are thieves of your crowns, wolves who like greedy dogs will deceive you into following idols of men (Isaiah 56).

2:19 Nevertheless the foundation of God standeth sure, having this seal, The Lord knoweth them that are his. And, **Let every one that nameth the name of Christ depart from iniquity.**

In the Ekklesia there are the zealous for God and the tares without the fruits of godliness: and then there are the blatant evil does who seek to lead us away from any zeal for godliness.

Jesus, Jude, Paul and others warn us that in these last days many false teachers will arise in the midst of the spiritual Ekklesia, to attempt to deceive us away from any zeal for godliness and to deceive us into following them as our idols of men.

2:20 But in a great house there are not only vessels of gold and of silver, but also of wood and of earth; and some to honour, and some to dishonour.

Reject and purge yourselves of these deceitful false teachers and embrace a wholehearted passionate zeal to learn and to live by every Word of God! In doing so we will internalize the true nature God and will become a fitting part of the collective spiritual bride!

2:21 If a man therefore purge himself from these, he shall be a vessel unto honour, sanctified, and meet for the master's use, and prepared unto every good work.

Flee all sin and wholeheartedly live by every Word of God and embrace all godly virtues.

2:22 Flee also youthful lusts: but follow righteousness, faith, charity, peace, with them that call on the Lord out of a pure [sincere, honest] heart. **2:23** But foolish and unlearned questions avoid, knowing that they do gender strifes.

2:24 And the servant of the Lord must not strive; but be gentle unto all men, apt to teach, patient, **2:25** In meekness instructing those that oppose themselves [Patiently warn those (especially in the brotherhood) who reject any zeal to learn and to live by every Word of God.]; if God peradventure will give them repentance to the acknowledging of the truth;

Help the brethren to recover themselves out of the snares of false teachers who encourage sin and compromise with any part of the whole Word of God; saying that Jesus is love and will understand and overlook willful sin, thereby falsely justifying sin and leading people to destruction.

2:26 And that they may recover themselves out of the snare of the devil, who are taken captive by him at his will.

2 Timothy 3

In Second Timothy 3, Paul issues a strong indictment against today's spiritual Ekklesia.

Paul directly warns us about the last days before Christ comes: Telling us what it will be like in the world and in the latter day spiritual Ekklesia.

These things all have their spiritual counterparts.

2 Timothy 3:1 This know also, that in the last days perilous times shall come. **3:2** For men shall be lovers of their own selves [selfish], covetous [loving to be preeminent], boasters [claiming great things and titles for themselves], proud, blasphemers, disobedient to parents [including being disobedient to God the Father], unthankful, unholy [not living by the Word of God],

The pride of today's religious leaders and elders in the spiritual Ekklesia [with very few exceptions] is enormous; each thinking that they know better than God and that their ways and false traditions trump the Word of God.

They blaspheme calling themselves God's people, when they teach and live in rebellion against the Word of God. They are rebellious against the Word of God and disobedient to the Word of God their Father. They are full of pride rejecting the holiness that comes from a passionate love and zeal for God to keep his Word.

They despise any zeal to keep God's Word having no love for godliness, loving only themselves and their own false traditions. They deceive the brethren into following idols of men, and falsely accuse the zealous for God of trying to divide the brethren, when it is they themselves who have divided the brethren from God and from each other.

3:3 Without natural affection, trucebreakers, false accusers, incontinent, fierce [combative and confrontational], despisers of those that are good

Jesus said; "only God is good" and that would include the whole Word of God as being good, which is the very nature of God,

Most of today's spiritual Ekklesia are traitors to their commitment to God the Father and to their baptismal covenant of espousal to Jesus Christ [Hebrew: Yeshua]; following idols of men and not following the Husband of their covenant of espousal.

3:4 Traitors, heady [intoxicated with their own ways, and filled with pride in themselves], highminded [arrogant and self-willed], **lovers of pleasures more than lovers of God;**

I have been directly told by people that they go to restaurants and profane God's holy Sabbath for their own personal pleasure. This is openly admitted! Today's spiritual Ekklesia loves their own pleasures instead of making the things of God their pleasure, as it is written.

> **Isaiah 58:13** If thou turn away thy foot from the sabbath, from doing thy pleasure on my holy day; and call the sabbath a delight, the holy of the Lord, honourable; and shalt honour him, **not doing thine own ways, nor finding thine own pleasure, nor speaking thine own words: 58:14** Then shalt thou delight thyself in the Lord; and I will cause thee to ride upon the high places of the earth, and feed thee with the heritage of Jacob thy father: for the mouth of the Lord hath spoken it.

Today's spiritual Ekklesia does their best to try to appear godly but in appearances only, making a pretense of keeping the Sabbath and High Days while polluting them.

We love to call ourselves "God's church" or "God's people;" which is a blasphemy because we are NOT God's people, but the people of the idols we follow. We are in rebellion against the Word of God by following idols of men, and by doing so we deny the authority [the power] of God.

2 Timothy 3:5 Having a form of godliness, but denying the power thereof: from such turn away.

Our leaders are our deceivers, creeping about to lead foolish and sinful brethren to follow idols of men.

Instead of rebuking all sin at all times, like a true godly elder would; they falsely teach that a little sin will be overlooked, and so entice the spiritually weak and foolish to continue in sin [and the vain pleasures of sin]; stealing their crowns!

3:6 For of this sort are they which creep into houses, and lead captive silly women [foolish women being a type of today's spiritual Ekklesia] laden with sins, led away with divers lusts,

These false elders and leaders present themselves as great scholars while never understanding the truth; because they will not submit themselves to the whole Word of God and instead try to force and twist God's Word to back up their own false teachings.

3:7 Ever learning, and never able to come to the knowledge of the truth.

Just as the magicians of Pharaoh resisted Moses, those who resist the Word of God today are spiritually corrupted into the gross error of their own ways, following idols of man and false traditions.

These Resisters of the Truth; self-justify following error, false traditions and sin and are reprobates from God's Word

3:8 Now as **Jannes and Jambres withstood Moses**, so do these also resist the truth: men of corrupt minds, reprobate concerning the faith. **3:9 But they shall proceed no further** [such men will not prosper, for Almighty God will rise up to correct them]: **for their folly shall be manifest** [revealed, made known] **unto all men, as their's** [Jannes and Jambres] **also was.**

All truly godly persons will suffer persecutions and often from their own household, including from the supposed spiritual Ekklesia. The seal of godliness is not wealth or numbers, but a zealous dedicated living by every Word of God.

3:10 But thou hast fully known my doctrine, manner of life, purpose, faith, longsuffering, charity, patience, **3:11** Persecutions, afflictions, which came unto me at Antioch, at Iconium, at Lystra; what persecutions I endured: but out of them all the Lord delivered me. **3:12 Yea, and all that will live godly in Christ Jesus shall suffer persecution.**

In the world and in today's Ekklesia, wicked deceivers and wickedness will continue to increase, deceiving many of the brethren away from our God and away from God's Word.

3:13 But evil men and seducers shall wax worse and worse, deceiving, and being deceived.

Brethren, prove all things by the whole Word of God and continue diligently in the Holy Scriptures.

3:14 But continue thou in the things which thou hast learned and hast been assured of, knowing of whom thou hast learned them; **3:15** And that **from a child thou hast known the holy scriptures, which are able to make thee wise unto salvation through faith which is in Christ Jesus.**

It is not enough to know the scriptures or to have faith; we must also have the works of faith and the works of godliness; diligently living by every Word of God.

3:16 All scripture is given by inspiration of God, and is profitable for doctrine, for reproof, for correction, for instruction in righteousness: 3:17 That the man of God may be perfect, throughly furnished unto all good works.

2 Timothy 4

Timothy and all elders and brethren are charged to be faithful to live by and to faithfully teach every Word of God

2 Timothy 4:1 I charge thee therefore before God, and the Lord Jesus Christ, who shall judge the quick and the dead at his appearing and his kingdom; **4:2 Preach the word; be instant in season, out of season; reprove, rebuke, exhort with all longsuffering and doctrine**.

Paul warns that most of the latter day spiritual Ekklesia will stray far from any zeal for sound doctrine and the Word of God, to follow false traditions [fables] and idols of men and corporate entities.

This supports Paul's statement to the Thessalonians that there will be a great falling away of the Ekklesia just before the tribulation.

4:3 For the time will come when they will not endure sound doctrine; but after their own lusts shall they heap to themselves teachers, having itching ears; 4:4 And they shall turn away their ears from the truth, and shall be turned unto fables.

Let the godly watch and be zealously faithful to live by every Word of God and be strong to endure anything and everything; to learn, to live by and to teach every Word of God.

Do not depart from following God the Father and our espoused Husband Jesus Christ to follow idols of men and false traditions

4:5 But watch thou in all things, endure afflictions, do the work of an evangelist, make full proof of thy ministry.

Paul, writing from Rome indicates that his judgment at court is very close and that he believes that he will soon die.

4:6 For I am now ready to be offered, and the time of my departure is at hand.

Let us all fight the good fight of faithfulness to our beloved LORD; so that we may all be delivered to the resurrection to spirit and eternal life by the true righteous judge.

4:7 I have fought a good fight, I have finished my course, I have kept the faith: **4:8** Henceforth there is laid up for me a crown of righteousness, which the Lord, the righteous judge, shall give me at that day: and not to me only, but unto all them also that love his appearing.

Paul asks Timothy to come quickly to him for his time is at hand.

4:9 Do thy diligence to come shortly unto me [in Rome]: **4:10** For Demas hath forsaken me, having loved this present world, and is departed unto Thessalonica; [Crescens and Titus have left but have not forsaken Paul, having gone to care for the churches; and so Paul was left with only Luke in Rome, at his time of judgment by the Emperor.] Crescens to Galatia, Titus unto Dalmatia.

Paul asks that his friends come to him and bring him his beloved books so that he may be comforted in his last months.

4:11 Only Luke is with me. Take Mark, and bring him with thee: for he is profitable to me for the ministry. **4:12** And Tychicus have I sent to Ephesus. **4:13** The cloke that I left at Troas with Carpus, when thou comest, bring with thee, and the books, but especially the parchments.

Timothy is warned to beware of adversaries just as we also should beware of those who would entice us with clever words to subvert our faith and zeal for God and the whole Word of God.

4:14 Alexander the coppersmith did me much evil: the Lord reward him according to his works: **4:15** Of whom be thou ware also; for he hath greatly withstood our words.

At Paul's first appearance before the Roman court he was abandoned by others of the faith and forced to stand alone. Paul gives his forgiveness for this abandonment.

4:16 At my first answer no man stood with me, but all men forsook me: I pray God that it may not be laid to their charge.

At his first hearing in Rome, although abandoned by his friends, Paul still found courage in Christ and gave a good witness of God's way to the court, and judgment was deferred. His witness to the court was then spread abroad to all of Rome, so that all in Rome heard of God's way.

4:17 Notwithstanding **the Lord stood with me, and strengthened me; that by me the preaching might be fully known, and that all the Gentiles might hear**: and I was delivered out of the mouth of the lion.

Paul then witnessed to Timothy and to us; that all those who stand steadfast in godliness will be delivered from every evil, to rise from the grave an eternal spirit with God.

4:18 And the Lord shall deliver me from every evil work, and will preserve me unto his heavenly kingdom: to whom be glory for ever and ever. Amen.

4:19 Salute Prisca and Aquila, and the household of Onesiphorus [Onesimus]. **4:20** Erastus abode at Corinth: but Trophimus have I left at Miletum sick.

Evidently this Epistle was written in summer and Paul asks Timothy to come before winter.

4:21 Do thy diligence to come before winter. Eubulus greeteth thee [greets Timothy], and Pudens, and Linus, and Claudia, and all the brethren.

4:22 The Lord Jesus Christ be with thy spirit. Grace be with you. Amen.

Titus

Titus 1

In his introduction Paul calls himself an apostle [messenger] of the Word of God, to whom was committed the preaching of the whole Word of God. He calls Titus his own son in the faith.

Titus 1:1 Paul, a servant of God, and an apostle of Jesus Christ, according to the faith of God's elect, and the acknowledging of the truth which is after godliness; **1:2** In hope of eternal life, which God, that cannot lie, promised before the world began; **1:3** But hath in due times manifested his word through preaching, which is committed unto me according to the commandment of God our Saviour; **1:4** To Titus, mine own son after the common faith: Grace, mercy, and peace, from God the Father and the Lord Jesus Christ our Saviour.

Paul had left Titus remaining in Crete for the purpose of establishing congregations in every city.

1:5 For this cause left I thee in Crete, that thou shouldest set in order the things that are wanting, and ordain elders in every city, as I had appointed thee:

Paul then begins to lay out for Titus [who was tasked with establishing congregations and ordaining elders in Crete] as he had to Timothy, the qualifications required in those acceptable for ordination as elders in the faith.

First they must be blameless according to the whole Word of God, pure from all sin so that they are a Shining Example to the brethren.

Second they must have proved their capability to lead by having one wife, [or having had a wife in the case of widowers], and by having older children who although they may not be called by God have still been raised wisely.

Let me say here that occasionally, especially in today's society immersed in so much wickedness, not all of our children will grow into moral adults. However if they have been encouraged and taught godliness [which is a real struggle since our modern education system teaches them to be wicked]; once they have experienced the sufferings of the dark side of life and are called by God in their due time they will be saved.

I know that many agonize over wayward children and other family members: however if we teach them godliness by our example and instruction we have the hope that in due time they will be saved by our Mighty God. This is about how the parent as a candidate for ordination, leans to teach godliness to the brethren by first teaching godliness to their children.

1:6 If any be blameless, the husband of one wife, having faithful children not accused of riot or unruly.

An elder must be blameless in the zealous keeping of the whole Word of God as a Shining Light of example for the brethren and for the worldly as well.

1:7 For a bishop must be blameless, as the steward of God; not selfwilled [stubborn], not soon angry, not given to wine, no striker, not given to filthy lucre;

Then the positive character qualities needed are listed.

1:8 But a lover of hospitality, a lover of good [wise in godliness] men, sober [moderate in all things], just [fair, balanced and not a respecter of persons in any matter], holy [zealous to live by every Word of God and to internalize the nature of God], temperate [moderate]; **1:9** Holding fast the faithful word [the whole Word of God] as he hath been taught [This does NOT refer to any corporate traditions; it refers to being taught the Holy

Scriptures and being fully grounded in sound doctrine.], **that he may be able by sound doctrine both to exhort and to convince the gainsayers.**

Even in Paul's day there were many false teachers creeping in and deceiving many brethren in the Ekklesia. This is a specific warning to Titus about Crete, however we are warned in many scriptures that this deceiving and falling away will increase until it climaxes among the latter day brethren.

1:10 For there are many unruly and vain talkers and deceivers, specially they of the circumcision: **1:11** Whose mouths must be stopped, who subvert whole houses, teaching things which they ought not, for filthy lucre's sake. **1:12** One of themselves, even a prophet [proper translation: a "poet"] of their own, said, The Cretians are alway liars, evil beasts, slow bellies.

True men of God are commanded to sharply rebuke all sin and willful sinners; especially those in the ministry who have a greater responsibility, being teachers of others.

1:13 This witness is true. Wherefore rebuke them sharply, that they may be sound in the faith;

All of God's called pout are called to become priests of God and teachers of godliness, yet some are intended as older brothers to help the brethren achieve that purpose. The job of leaders, elders and teachers is to keep the brethren focused on God and godliness; God's called out must never follow the false traditions of men or fall into the idolatry of allowing men to come between us and God.

God's called out are NOT to follow any deceivers who teach anything contrary to the whole Word of God, like many of today's leaders in the spiritual Ekklesia who teach the brethren to follow themselves and to reject any zeal to live by every Word of God (Mat 4:4).

1:14 Not giving heed to Jewish fables, and commandments of men, that turn from the truth.

True godliness means never accepting the non-scriptural traditions of any person or organization.

1:15 Unto the pure [godly] all [godly] things are pure: but unto them that are defiled [by wickedness and rejection of zeal to keep God's Word] and unbelieving is nothing pure [the mind of the wicked person is unclean and impure]; but even their mind and conscience is defiled.

Here Paul absolutely accurately describes today's called out brethren, who call the Sabbath holy as they trample all over it, rejecting any zeal to live by every Word of God in order to follow idols of men.

1:16 They profess that they know God; but in works they deny him, being abominable, and disobedient, and unto every good work reprobate.

Titus 2

This is what the elders are commanded to teach the brethren. First the sound doctrine of the Holy Scriptures is to be taught to and followed by everyone.

Titus 2:1 But speak thou the things which become sound doctrine: **2:2** That the aged **men** be sober [self-controlled], grave [serious], temperate [moderate], sound in [full of] faith [which includes the works of faith], in charity [Godly love which is the zealous keeping of every Word of God.], in patience.

Older women are to teach the younger women to be self-controlled, and to teach them how to love others more than themselves.

2:3 The aged women likewise, that they be in behaviour as becometh holiness [godliness], not false accusers, not given to much wine, **teachers** [the women are to teach, yet they are not to usurp the authority of their men] of good things [being teachers of all things consistent with godliness and God's Word]; **2:4** That they may teach the young women to be sober [self-controlled], to love their husbands, to love their children [to be unselfish and caring], **2:5** To be discreet, chaste, keepers at home [this refers to avoiding wantonness and not to gainful work with the husband's consent], good [godly], obedient to their own husbands, that the word of God be not blasphemed.

They are to set a godly example so that others may see their Light Shine; instead of setting a bad example while claiming to be godly and thus causing others to say evil things about God and this way.

2:6 Young men likewise exhort to be sober minded [to be self-controlled and full of the mind of God].

The elders are to be a pattern [example of godliness] demonstrating the works of faith, standing on and living by the sound doctrine of the whole Word of God without any corruption of error.

2:7 In all things shewing thyself a pattern of good works: in doctrine shewing uncorruptness, [without any hint of corruption or false teachings] gravity, sincerity, **2:8** Sound speech [sound words consistent with the whole Word of God], that cannot be condemned [by God]; that he that is of the contrary part may be [ultimately] ashamed [when his eyes are opened, having no evil thing to say of you.

2:9 Exhort servants to be obedient unto their own masters, and to please them well in all things; not answering again [not arguing or resisting authority as long as they are not being told to sin]; **2:10** Not purloining [stealing], but shewing all good fidelity [loyalty]; that they may adorn [be a Shining Example of godliness] the doctrine of God our Saviour in all things.

2:11 For the grace [forgiveness of repented PAST sins, through the sacrifice of Christ] of God that bringeth salvation hath appeared [will be revealed in due time] to all men,

We are to reject all worldliness and sin, and we are to continue in godly living for our salvation at the coming of Christ.

2:12 Teaching us that, denying ungodliness [we must reject all things which are contrary to any part of the whole Word of God] and worldly lusts [temptations], we should live soberly [with self-control], righteously [zealously living by every Word of God], and godly, in this present world;

2:13 Looking for that blessed hope, and the glorious appearing of the great God and our Saviour Jesus Christ; **2:14** Who gave himself for us, that he might redeem us from all iniquity, **and purify unto himself a peculiar people** [a special set apart people, made pure from all sin], **zealous of good works** [the good works of faith are to learn and to live by every Word of God].

True men of God will teach these things fearlessly, rebuking all sin without any hint of compromise; by the authority of Almighty God, knowing that godliness is our salvation.

2:15 These things speak, and exhort, and rebuke with all authority. Let no man despise thee.

Titus 3

Obey all godly, lawful, laws of man; and do not be given to fighting, nevertheless do take a stand on God's Word and do rebuke all sin.

Titus 3:1 Put them in mind to be subject to principalities and powers, to obey magistrates, to be ready to [do] every good work [live consistent with godliness], **3:2** To speak evil [condemn] of no man, to be no brawlers, but gentle, shewing all meekness unto all men.

3:3 For we ourselves also were sometimes foolish, disobedient, deceived, serving divers lusts and pleasures, living in malice and envy, hateful, and hating one another.

We are called out of sin by the mercy of God, and if we sincerely repent of our past sins and commit to "sin no more," our PAST sins are paid for and our indictment is swept clean by the application of the sacrifice of Christ! From that moment forward as we rise from baptism a new person, we are to diligently root out all sin, learning and living by every Word of God.

We are justified by the mercy of God, and we are to go forward into godliness by learning and keeping the whole Word of God just as Jesus Christ did: Never turning back into the bondage of sin that God has mercifully delivered us out of.

3:4 But after that the kindness and love of God our Saviour toward man appeared, **3:5 Not by works of righteousness which we have done, but**

according to his mercy he saved us, by the washing of regeneration, and renewing of the Holy Ghost; **3:6** Which he shed on us abundantly through Jesus Christ our Saviour; **3:7** That being justified by his grace, we should be made heirs according to the hope of eternal life.

3:8 This is a faithful saying, and these things I will that thou affirm constantly, that **they which have believed in God might be careful to maintain good works** [Good works are the works of faith and godliness, which is living by every Word of God.]. These things are good and profitable unto men.

Avoid arguing about insignificant things

3:9 But avoid foolish questions, and genealogies, and contentions, and strivings about the law [A reference to the conflicts between the Jews and the Gentiles over various Jewish non scriptural traditions like weekly fasting's, refusing to enter a Gentile convert's home, the circumcision controversy and the other issues that Paul had been forced to deal with. Paul is informing Timothy that these things had been dealt with and were not to be debated any further.]; for they are unprofitable and vain [a waste of time].

The sinful [especially sinful elders] are to be warned and counseled, instructed and gently admonished the first time. The second time they are to be rebuked and warned that after another such sin they will be expelled. Then if they try to justify their sin or their sin continues, they are to be expelled from the assemblies until they sincerely repent and stop the sin; and if they sincerely repent and stop the sin they should then be forgiven and welcomed back into the assembly.

Elders who have justified their sins and rejected godliness should be rejected from being elders.

3:10 A man that is an heretick after the first and second admonition reject; 3:11 Knowing that he that is such is subverted, and sinneth, being condemned of himself.

Paul is writing from Nicopolis

3:12 When I shall send Artemas unto thee, or Tychicus, be diligent to come unto me to Nicopolis: for **I have determined there to winter**. **3:13** Bring Zenas the lawyer and Apollos on their journey diligently, that nothing be wanting unto them.

All of the brethren are encouraged to be full of the good works of godliness and faith.

3:14 And let our's [all the brethren] also learn to maintain good works [living by the works of faith and godliness] for necessary uses, that they be not unfruitful.

3:15 All that are with me salute thee. Greet them that love us in the faith. Grace be with you all. Amen.

Philemon

Philemon

Paul wrote to Philemon to reconcile Onesimus with Philemon

Philemon had heard Paul teach and had apparently told his servant Onesimus about Paul. Onesimus was so impressed with Philemon's reports about Paul's teachings that he had straightway thoughtlessly ran off to find Paul without informing his master.

This epistle is an example of lovingly seeking to reconcile brethren who have been offended by one another.

Paul sent Onesimus back to Philemon at Colossae with Tychicus who was also delivering the Epistle from Paul to the Colossians.

> **Colossians 4:7** All my state shall Tychicus declare unto you, who is a beloved brother, and a faithful minister and fellowservant in the Lord: **4:8** Whom I have sent unto you for the same purpose, that he might know your estate, and comfort your hearts; **4:9** With Onesimus, a faithful and beloved brother, who is one of you. They shall make known unto you all things which are done here.

Paul writing from Rome was imprisoned for preaching Christ; this does not mean that Paul was calling himself a prisoner held by Christ; he was the prisoner of the Romans having appealed to Caesar because of the false accusations made about him.

Philemon 1:1 Paul, a prisoner of Jesus Christ, and Timothy our brother, unto Philemon our dearly beloved, and fellowlabourer, **1:2** And to our beloved Apphia, and Archippus our fellowsoldier, and to the church in thy house: **1:3** Grace to you, and peace, from God our Father and the Lord Jesus Christ.

Paul begins by referring to the deep conversion of Philemon, so as to gently remind Philemon of his obligation to forgive others.

1:4 I thank my God, making mention of thee always in my prayers, **1:5** Hearing of thy love and faith, which thou hast toward the Lord Jesus, and toward all saints; **1:6** That the communication of thy faith may become effectual by the acknowledging of every good thing which is in you in Christ Jesus. **1:7** For we have great joy and consolation in thy love, because the bowels of the saints are refreshed by thee, brother.

Paul says that he could command Philemon, but that he thinks it much more appropriate to beseech him as a friend and brother in regards to this matter, because after all Onesimus was the one in the wrong.

1:8 Wherefore, though I might be much bold in Christ to enjoin thee that which is convenient, **1:9** Yet for love's sake I rather beseech thee, being such an one as Paul the aged, and now also a prisoner of Jesus Christ.

Paul explained that Philemon's servant Onesimus had left him to seek out Paul and was now converted in the faith; and that Onesimus who had been unprofitable to Philemon by leaving his master without seeking his consent; was now very profitable in the faith.

Paul asks Philemon to accept Onesimus as he would accept Paul himself.

1:10 I beseech thee for my son Onesimus, whom I have begotten in my bonds: **1:11** Which in time past was to thee unprofitable, but now profitable to thee and to me: **1:12** Whom I have sent again: thou therefore receive him, that is, mine own bowels:

Paul then praises Onesimus for his service to Paul, but sends him back so as to allow Philemon to decide for himself what is to be done concerning his own servant.

1:13 Whom I would have retained with me, that in thy stead he might have ministered unto me in the bonds of the gospel: **1:14** But without thy mind would I do nothing; that thy benefit should not be as it were of necessity, but willingly.

Paul told Philemon that if he considers himself in the faith, he will forgive Onesimus and accept him as a brother in the faith.

1:15 For perhaps he therefore departed for a season, that thou shouldest receive him for ever; **1:16** Not now as a servant, but above a servant, a brother beloved, specially to me, but how much more unto thee, both in the flesh, and in the Lord? **1:17** If thou count me therefore a partner [if you are my brother in the same faith], receive him as myself.

1:18 If he hath wronged thee, or oweth thee ought, put that on mine account; **1:19** I Paul have written it with mine own hand, I will repay it: albeit I do not say to thee how thou owest unto me even thine own self besides.

Paul declares his confidence in the conversion and love of Philemon, that he would forgive Onesimus and accept as a brother in the faith..

1:20 Yea, brother, let me have joy of thee in the Lord: refresh my bowels in the Lord. **1:21** Having confidence in thy obedience I wrote unto thee, knowing that thou wilt also do more than I say.

Paul indicates that he will soon be coming to Colosse and will visit Philemon and Onesimus then.

1:22 But withal prepare me also a lodging: for I trust that through your prayers I shall be given unto you.

1:23 There salute thee Epaphras, my fellowprisoner in Christ Jesus; **1:24** Marcus, Aristarchus, Demas, Lucas, my fellowlabourers.

1:25 The grace [mercy, forgiveness] of our Lord Jesus Christ be with your spirit. Amen.

Visit Our Website
theshininglight.info

www.ingramcontent.com/pod-product-compliance
Lightning Source LLC
Chambersburg PA
CBHW081147230426
43664CB00018B/2830